Return
of the
Lost Son

Return
of the
Lost Son

MEMORIES OF
MY WAYWARD FATHER

CHRISTOPHER
GONZALES

LOUISIANA STATE UNIVERSITY PRESS
BATON ROUGE

Published by Louisiana State University Press
lsupress.org

LSU Press Paperback Original

Designer: Kaelin Chappell Broaddus
Typefaces: Dolly Pro, text; Acumin Pro, display

Cover illustration: Adobe Stock/fran_kie.

Cataloging-in-Publication Data are available from the Library of Congress.
ISBN 978-0-8071-8469-1 (paperback) | ISBN 978-0-8071-8543-8 (epub) |
ISBN 978-0-8071-8544-5 (pdf)

for Jenny
and Mateo and Joseph, our sons

Love is so short, forgetting is so long.

—PABLO NERUDA

What matters in life is not what happens to you
but what you remember and how you remember it.

—GABRIEL GARCÍA MÁRQUEZ

CONTENTS

This book portrays the memories of nearly two dozen individuals. All of the characters and events in this story are real. Some names have been changed to protect identities, or to avoid confusion between characters.

Return
of the
Lost Son

Return of the Lost Son

In the summer of 1988, I was riding in a car with my family, some-where in Texas. In the back seat, I leaned my head against the window, watching the mile markers sailing past. I was sixteen years old. Beyond the wavering shoulder of the road, the orange-brown prairie grasses rippled. The tires hummed along the highway. The engine was running smoothly, and we had a full tank of gas. The day was burning, and bright, intense sunlight invaded the car.

My father, fifty-three years old, wore 1930s classic aviator sunglasses as he drove our station wagon. In the front, my mother fumbled with a map. My sister Heather, nineteen, had hung a Grateful Dead T-shirt over the window, folded and pinched between the rolled-up window and frame, to block the relentless sun. Like my father, I wore sunglasses, but mine were futuristic, wraparound.

As I looked through the window at the prairie grasses, thoughts repeated in my mind: This was the trip to find my father's parents. He hadn't seen them in twenty-five years. We'd been traveling for several days since leaving our home in upstate New York. We had hours to go before we would reach our destination: Austin, my father's hometown.

The car turned, our bodies swayed. As the engine noise dropped, the tires bumped on the gravel of the off-ramp.

"Rene, why did you exit?" my mother asked my father.

"This is the way we're all going."

She said she didn't understand, stop the car. We all looked at my father. My mother leaned toward him. My father seemed to think every exit was his exit. Every time he came to an exit, he took it. We pulled into a gas station parking lot. The engine cut. Cars clacked over the pavement gaps of the off-ramp.

"Are you all right?" She looked at him with concern.

Everyone got out of the car. I stood and stretched my numb legs. Several yards away, on the other side of the car, my mother was clutching the map, in tense conversation with my father, but I couldn't hear. She seemed impatient, exasperated; he seemed bewildered. A few minutes later, Heather returned from the mini market carrying a cup of cold soda. My mother announced it was time to go and she was driving.

"Where are my sunglasses?" I said. I opened the rear passenger door and looked inside. They were gone.

"Dad's looking for his sunglasses," Heather said, gesturing toward him with her cup.

"No, wait, it's me," I said. "*I'm* looking for my sunglasses." I opened the front passenger door now, bending inside, and began rummaging through the clutter of paper napkins, guidebooks, and maps. I'd left them right on the seat. Where had they gone?

I stood up. The distant roar of the highway came closer, then swirled in my head. Stars crossed my periphery. I was still standing, yet I sensed I'd just woken up. My father was walking around the car, toward me on the passenger side. He was a slender man with prominent cheekbones, a bump on the bridge of his nose, his hair curled and streaked with distinguished gray. He was wearing my sunglasses.

I could see myself in those sunglasses at that moment: a tiny, funhouse-mirror warped silhouette. My father looked like an aged version of me, or a ghost from the future, *me* as a father who'd traveled back in time to visit my younger self. If my father was lost, so was I. I tried to make sense of what was happening to him, to us, recalling hints from the last few days of our travel together. He muddled his words. He answered my questions with, "I don't remember," "I'm not

2

sure," or "I don't recall." He couldn't find his keys, his cigarette lighter, or the right map. These clues were gradually coalescing into a larger idea. It crept around in the back of my mind. When I saw him wearing my sunglasses, it crawled to the front. Something was wrong with my father's perception. Something was wrong with my father's mind.

><+→+<

With my mother driving the car, and my father now relegated to the passenger seat, we came to a broken-down neighborhood in Austin. Through the car windows I saw boarded-up storefronts, scrawls of graffiti, broken glass, cassette tape streamers, and tall grass growing through cracked sidewalks. I'd never met my paternal grandparents, and I kept expecting my father would say, "We're here," and they would be huddled among the tough men holding paper bags in the shadows.

The next day we visited the campus of the University of Texas at Austin, and I sat beneath the winding oaks. Did my grandparents come here, under the trees? In an open field on the campus, I glimpsed a blacktail jackrabbit: long, black-tipped ears, a brown and shaggy body, and large rear legs. I needed then to see the jackrabbit more clearly, to understand it, to marvel at it. I wanted to learn something about this animal that looks so similar but was still so different from the rabbits I was used to seeing in the Northeast. Meanwhile my family was hurrying to our car in the parking lot, asking why I seemed to be daydreaming.

Another day we walked inside the grand Texas Capitol. My mother told a story of my father, as a teenager, a Mexican American page, one of the first, an aspiring political leader, running administrative paperwork through the building's corridors. I wondered whether my father's ancestors appeared in the building's murals of democracy, of the Republic of Texas, of its independence day in 1836.

Austin's mix of skyscrapers, low brick buildings, cactuses, riverfront, fluorescent billboards, and Tex-Mex restaurants tugged at my imagination. I so badly wanted to understand my father, his family,

Texas, and Austin. But as we walked around the popular tourist sites, I cringed, feeling like an outsider and a failure. We had traveled halfway across the United States. But what I remember was my father approaching me in the wraparound sunglasses, something not quite right about him.

>}~~}{

Andrés, my father once told me, was a tough father, a bitter drinker, and an angry man.

My curiosity about my grandfather Andrés began long before I learned of his death. When I was growing up, my father seemed to want to forget his own father.

When Andrés's mother was pregnant with him, around the beginning of the Mexican Revolution, she crossed from Mexico into the United States. As a youth, Andrés kept his American citizenship, yet crossed back into Mexico. He and his beloved, my grandmother Minnie, knew each other growing up together in Burgos, Mexico. When I was seventeen and hearing these stories for the first time, I kept getting lost in the complications. Only much later could I tell the story of how my grandparents came together, giving me a sense of meaning amid the quiet of my father's failing memory and denial of his history.

Andrés was born in Brownsville, Texas, on November 30, 1910: ten days after wealthy liberal politician Francisco Madero announced his opposition to despotic president Porfirio Díaz and called for a national uprising. The violent convulsions quickly spread across the country and marked the start of the Mexican Revolution. Around this time thousands of Mexican refugees who had lived in the northeastern Mexican provinces of Chihuahua, Coahuila, Nuevo León, and Tamaulipas crossed the ill-defined border northward to Texas, seeking the political stability and economic promise of the United States.

In an instant, I see the mother of Andrés, riding in a wagon with her husband, her white dress stretched over her swollen belly. The air is cool and pleasant in the late morning. She and her husband travel in a caravan of horses, buggies, and carts, rumbling in the dust and rocks on the dirt road. They arrive at the Rio Grande, called by Mexicans the Río Bravo del Norte. It is late afternoon and the overhanging trees cast long shadows over the muddy green water. The river at this geographic point is nothing more than an arroyo, a trifle, a rivulet a few dozen yards wide, set between shallow embankments.

The mother of Andrés, with her bulging tummy and her feet stinging like nettles, dips her feet into the water. She takes one or two cautious steps, slipping herself into the stream. Her skirts float up as the river swirls and eddies around them.

"Mi amor, el bebé viene," the mother of Andrés cries. "My love, the baby is coming."

In the hospital in Brownsville, the mother of Andrés holds the infant, who coos and gurgles softly.

>+••+<

In Austin in 1988, my family and I wandered through the city like tourists. We'd traveled 1,840 miles from upstate New York to reunite with our grandparents and got no farther than a few places on the map from the tourist office. It was as if we'd come all that way to find a blacktail jackrabbit, and the creature darted in and out of the shrubs on the edge of the field, then slipped away, through the bushes. The understanding I'd wanted of my father was as elusive as this wild animal, out of place on a university campus.

I know my father truly wanted to find his parents. He flipped through the Austin phone book, finding so many people named Gonzales, unlike upstate New York, where we were the only ones. He couldn't find the names of his mother, father, or siblings. He didn't know whether his parents were alive or dead. "We've driven around different neighborhoods for two afternoons, and I don't want to do it again," my mother said with exasperation. A quiet thief had been slipping jewels from my father's memory. My father couldn't remember the name of the street where he had lived. And we didn't find his parents.

>+++<

Less than a month after we returned to Middle Grove, his family found *him*. As a kid, I knew my father had three children by his first marriage, and even imagined one day somebody would find us. Sure enough, one evening, the phone rang, and I answered it.

"Hello, is Joe there?" a woman asked in a hesitant voice. "I'm trying to find Joe Gonzales."

I knew something was odd because only people from a long time ago would call my father Joe. We called him Rene. She said her name was Alexis. She suspected she'd found her dad. She believed she and I were brother and sister. I had a strange feeling, because I'd always expected this phone call. She was calling from Oklahoma City. She'd been looking for her father for nineteen years. He had family in Austin looking for him.

"We just drove to Austin," I said.

"His mother lives in the same house as she did when he left," she said. "But Austin has changed a lot."

I didn't mention we were beginning to see failings in my father's memory.

She said my dad got a speeding ticket in Virginia. That's how she found him. I told her we got pulled over on our drive back from Texas. My dad was driving sixty miles per hour where the speed limit was fifty-five. My sister Heather said the Virginia State Police had singled us out because she'd hung a Grateful Dead T-shirt in the car window.

"Is your father home?" Alexis asked. "Could I speak with him?"

My father was sitting at the kitchen table, working on the *New York Times* crossword puzzle. He loved crosswords and liked to use their eccentric words and phrases; he often told me my behavior was *uncouth*. He insisted that I must respect my schoolteacher as though the rules were *sacrosanct*. He said that I was made of *sterner stuff*, recalling our time practicing my lines in the sixth-grade play, an excerpt of *Julius Caesar*. But when I handed him the phone with his daughter Alexis on the line, what I heard was muffled and almost silent.

"Yes, I'm Joe Gonzales," he said. It sounded strange. This designation was a bridge to his past, and I wanted to cross it. He said he'd just taken a trip to Texas to try to find his parents. Oh, he winced. Just like that, he winced. It was quick as a pinprick. He cleared his throat and said, "I had a feeling my father had died."

I left the room. I wanted to stay and listen to my father's half of the conversation, but I felt I was a trespasser into my father's hidden life, an interloper. Even though my father didn't ask me to leave, the news of his own father's death made me weak. I walked away to give him privacy with his daughter. Once, when I asked my father what he wanted for his birthday, he said he wanted to be left alone. I understood this to mean he wanted neither to receive nor to give back. I responded with my own silence. When I heard my grandfather, whom I'd never known, had died, I gave my father his distance. I didn't touch him, I didn't comfort him. But I knew we would go back to Austin and finally meet the rest of his family. The clarity I'd wanted regarding his family would come. That night, Alexis would telephone the Gonzales family in Austin and bring them all into our lives.

One by one—first Uncle Gus, then Aunt Mary, then Aunt Jeanne, then Uncle Jaime—his brothers and sisters telephoned to welcome the return of my father.

I'm working hard to remember how the next pieces of the story fit together. The year was 1988. The birthday of Rene's mother was approaching. On June 17 she would be seventy-eight years old, and her children planned a large family gathering. My father immediately flew by himself to Austin, where the family reunion and birthday party took place. I later saw a videotape in which Rene, unbeknownst to his mother, Minnie, had come. He stood before her. She grasped her chest, as if suffering a heart attack, a serious one. Someone offered her a chair and she sat down, stunned, mouth opening and closing, almost in tears, slowly fanning herself. As I watched this tape, it seemed cruel to me that they did not let her know Rene was coming.

In the summer of 1989, one year after we'd chased the jackrabbit in Austin, my father, mother, sister, and I drove to Texas a second time.

When my grandfather Andrés was four years old, the revolutionary hostilities moved southward toward central Mexico. As a semblance of peace returned to the northern provinces, in the United States increased political pressure came to push immigrants in border towns back into Mexico. In 1914–15 hundreds of people of Mexican ancestry were persecuted and killed by Texas Rangers in poorly organized border patrols. During this wave of border violence, many immigrants returned southward to their native towns in Mexico. Andrés retained his American citizenship and in the mid-1910s he and his family returned to the town called Burgos in Tamaulipas, Mexico.

The woman who would become Andrés's wife and lifelong companion, Manuelita "Minnie" Villafuerte, was born in Taft, Texas, in 1911. Her family also claimed ties to Burgos. I heard family stories: Burgos was a rural paradise. The families of Minnie and Andrés spent much time there together.

In a reverie of mine, Andrés and Minnie, adolescents, are swimming in a tributary stream to the Conchos River, under the shelter of leafy trees. Their white garments, which keep them cool in the sun, cling to their bodies. They splash, make rapid strokes with their arms, and turn in the water, laughing.

"Tengo el cinturón," Andrés sputters, closing his fist around the cloth belt, pulling it from her waist. He waves it just out of Minnie's reach.

"¡Dámelo!" she shouts, her skirts floating in a cloud on the water's surface.

Eventually Andrés and Minnie would leave Burgos for the United States, go their separate ways, and meet again in Kingsville, Texas.

In a photograph from this time, the youthful Andrés is poised in a pinstriped suit, conservatively fastened with all three buttons. He wears a broad tie with a tight knot. In his left hand he holds a cigarette. His head is tilted, relaxed, giving him a sophisticated air. Minnie, in her twenties, shines like a movie star, a flapper. She stands in a white dress with her hand on her hip, insouciant. The long sleeves are drawn at the wrist, with a black ribbon on the cuff. Three ruffled skirts drop just below her knee. Her expression is confident and coy. A curl of her hair is pressed to her forehead. The square neck of her dress opens to the collarbone. Three glossy ribbons encircle the collar. A shell necklace sparkles. Her face reveals her youth, but she seems to desire a greater authority of age.

Andrés repeatedly asked Minnie to marry him, but each time she refused. Then, when a family tragedy struck, it prompted Andrés to marry another woman. Her name was Anita Canamar.

It was a marriage, Jeanne suggested, Andrés had rushed into. In 1929, his own mother, Dolores, at age fifty-eight, and sister, Tomascita, suddenly died (the sister in childbirth and his mother shortly thereafter from heartbreak). Andrés was nineteen and thrown into extreme grief. He went on a drinking binge for days, falling into a stupor. When he came to clarity, he couldn't remember when or where his mother was buried. Anita, an employee at the Singer Sewing Machine Company where he worked, promised to take care of him. They soon married and settled into family life. By this marriage they had two children, Dolores and Yolanda. But the marriage didn't last. As Aunt Jeanne put it, "his marriage to Anita was doomed because he could not forget my momma." When the marriage failed, Andrés again pursued Minnie.

Minnie's mother, Martina, at first had supported her daughter's refusal to marry. But when her husband (Minnie's father) died, her mother, herself alone, was in a difficult position to care for her four children. Meanwhile Andrés wouldn't accept this refusal of marriage. Martina reminded Minnie, twenty-one, that times had been hard for them since her father passed away. Andrés persisted, and eventually

Minnie agreed to marry him; they were wed on February 12, 1933, in Kingsville.

In 1933 the city of Kingsville dominated the Rio Grande valley as the main economic power in South Texas. Set near the Santa Gertrudis Creek, the city supported the sprawling livestock, cotton, and land enterprise of the King Ranch. On November 6, 1934, in Kingsville, Minnie, with Andrés outside the room, gave birth to their first child, a boy. They named him Jose Rene Gonzales.

Andrés traveled frequently with his wife and family in southern Texas, and as a result his children were born in different towns. As I grasped the names and birthplaces, they read like a book of the Old Testament: *Now Benjamin begat Bela his firstborn.* Jose Rene, in Kingsville in 1934; Mary Silvia, in Raymondville in 1937; Gustavo Homer, in Lockhart in 1939; Alejandro, in Taylor in 1940; Margaret Jeanne, in Taylor in 1942; Graciela, in Taylor in 1944; Jaime, in Austin in 1950.

In Austin in 1989, our family station wagon came to a stop in front of the low-slung ranch house on Schieffer Street. On the front lawn of my grandmother's house I had my first glimpse of my Austin relatives. *He had broken contact with them for twenty-five years.* Men wore formal business suits and ties; women wore frilly blouses and breezy skirts. I turned red with embarrassment in my khaki shorts and T-shirt as this family encircled us and welcomed us with a respectful awe. My father climbed out of the car, slowly, unsteadily walking toward the house of his mother. My Austin relatives pulled me in after him.

There were so many uncles, aunts, and cousins I couldn't keep them straight. I kept coming up with mnemonics like Uncle Alex had thick glasses, Uncle Gus had wise, thoughtful eyes, Uncle Jaime had the round face of a boy, Aunt Graciela was thin and reserved, Aunt Jeanne was spirited and warm, and my cousin Gloria looked like a fashion model. Her sister Gina had energy like a whip. Then there were the confusingly named twins, my cousins Diana and Deanna, in their twenties. Aunt Mary had a down-to-earth charm.

I lowered myself onto the lavender fabric of my grandmother's sofa. My cousins pulled chairs into a semicircle around me and settled into them, studying me with curiosity. I had an urge to blurt out questions. At the same time I wanted to sit quietly and observe everyone without drawing attention to myself. As it was, I already seemed to occupy the center of attention. We were the ones who'd come all the way from New York. The first thing I could think of to ask: So, how hot does it get here? Then: Do you eat cereal for breakfast? And: How long was Texas independent? Do you like milk? Are you rebels? Do you play an instrument? What time does school start? How often do you have these big family gatherings? Of all the questions and stories, my cousins said they wanted to learn about Uncle Rene, but their sentences always turned back to our grandfather Andrés. I said I wanted to learn about Andrés, but every sentence of mine stopped when I thought of their Uncle Rene, who had been lost for so long but had returned.

I'd always thought of my father as all-American. He spoke English with a broadcaster's accent. He looked like everybody else to me. We spoke only English at home. I suppose I'd never thought of my father as Tejano, or Mexican American, until I went to Austin and was surrounded by all of his Tejano relatives. I tried to see something Spanish, Arab, or Native American in the shape of their eyes and skin and hair color. I heard snippets of Spanish, which before then I'd heard only in a classroom. The house was ornately decorated. A lacquer cabinet with gold details contained a silver ornamental tea set. I was struck by the Catholic art: crucifixes, a print reproduction of Leonardo's *Last Supper*, and angels. Seraphim visited me. White cherubim with wings, blue-eyed and blonde messengers, spirits of imitation ivory and onyx, and guardian angels all called on me. For an instant I saw a young woman, with dark skin, wearing a blue cape, surrounded by light, speaking to me in a strange tongue. A mechanical clock played "Ave María." I'd been raised going to a Methodist church whose main adornment was a barren wooden cross towering over simple pews and empty walls, lit by stained glass windows, and I was unaccustomed to theatrical religious artworks.

We must've spent five or six nights in a hotel, visiting my grandmother's house each day. The first morning my grandmother Minnie brought into the dining room a tray of colorful *pan dulce*, sweet breads coated in dusty pink and yellow powdered sugar. Minnie had an air of sweet-tempered formality, a kindness I could see beyond her pale skin, curls of sea mist hair, and large circular glasses. The first day, for lunch, she offered me a *tamale hecho a mano*, a handmade tamale, which I accepted. She looked on approvingly as I unwrapped the corn husk from the doughy mass inside. The tamale tasted savory, filled with slow-cooked pork, onion, garlic, and chili.

"Te pareces tanto a Jose Rene," Minnie said, as if touched by a painful memory. She said I looked so much like "Jose Rene," the name she used for my father. This designation was another bridge to my father's past. At that moment I believed I somehow shared blame with my father for having broken contact with her for twenty-five years. I was part of the family that prevented him from returning to Austin. She'd lost her son, and I was the one who'd kept him. I was the child of an Anglo woman and my father. I was witnessing not only a family feud but a cultural war between Anglos and Mexicans. Even though she'd welcomed me into her home, I was one who'd trespassed. I found it hard not to think of Minnie as regarding me with love but still struggling to suppress feelings of rejection.

Once during the reunion I was alone with my grandmother Minnie in the kitchen. She was telling me a story in Spanish, because I told her I was taking Spanish in school, but I couldn't quite understand the words. They were lost to me. I wondered if because of a hearing loss she couldn't understand me. All I could catch was a whisper, repeating, "Mi hijo, mi hijo," "My son, my son," with unease. I had the impression she was telling a story of her child who went away and did not come back for twenty-five years. But perhaps instead she spoke about her son who *returned*, as I saw him, with something wrong with him, with his unsteady steps, his long periods of silence, his confused statements about time, location, and memory. Instead of her son returning home, a ghost who was barely able to speak or remember had come to haunt her. I have few impressions of the Austin family reunion as strong as those of my ghostly father.

I imagined throwing my arms around Minnie, saying, "Pero regresó," "But he came back," as if to console her. But I didn't actually do any such thing. Instead, I stood there in confused silence, reminding myself I was the one taking high school Spanish, wanting to understand my father, Mexico, Austin, and our family.

A year later, when I was in college, my mother called to tell me my father, at age fifty-six, had gone to see a neurologist. The doctors had ruled out everything else. No tumor. No encephalitis. No brain injury. No stroke. They'd done all the tests. Probable Alzheimer's was the only thing left. I was nineteen years old when he was diagnosed. My mother recorded in her diary the date when she learned of the diagnosis: September 11, 1991. She told me my father was making jumbled statements about the present, about the distant past. But he was speaking, was walking, was dressing himself, and was finding his way to the bathroom.

In 1997 he was admitted to Fort Hudson, a full-time care facility for patients with Alzheimer's. On November 12, the day of his admission, he could no longer speak, no longer dress himself, and no longer find his way to the bathroom.

His mother Minnie died in Austin in 1998.

I tell you these dates because with them I anchor myself in time and place and memory. My search and my story started in Austin in 1988, taking wrong turns on a highway, losing my sunglasses, and finding my father wearing them. In an open field on the University of Texas campus I tracked a blacktail jackrabbit. I know it was a blacktail because it was grayish brown with a black tail and rump and black-tipped ears. The jackrabbit slipped away into the bushes. Yet one year later, I was back in Austin, among Tejano princesses and guardian angels.

In 2009, I was working in my office in Ithaca, New York. I was thirty-seven years old. My mother called to say she was drawing up a living will for my father. He was losing his ability to swallow his food. He might not live much longer.

All at once, the floor beneath me fell away. The blacktail jackrabbit was darting back and forth, going round and round, in and out of the bushes. The angels, the cherubim and the seraphim, were flying, throwing rose petals. A *susurro*, a delicate noise, sounded like, "sometimes, sometimes." A Roman citizen sang out, "*Poor soul! his eyes are red as fire with weeping.*" Cousin Gloria was saying, "We have these big family gatherings all the time." I sensed I was losing consciousness, but I pulled out of it.

I was the survivor after my father's illness. As my father and his memory gradually disappeared, I gathered family stories, photographs, and letters. In my late twenties I began writing in notebooks almost every day. I couldn't stand losing my father to Alzheimer's and dreaded the idea that he'd be lost without a word or a trace. I wrote in order to make my life of losing him bearable.

I was overwhelmed as we started to notice my father was getting sick on our trip to Austin. In the joy of meeting his mother Minnie in Texas, despite her encroaching deafness, which meant we often couldn't understand each other, I found reasons for hope. Angels circled in Grandma's house. The pain of her deafness and my father's memory loss saddened me, but years later, it pleased me to think of my father and Minnie. Putting those memories into words strengthened me. If I had to tell you one thing to remember about visiting Austin, it's this. Don't feel so bad when the jackrabbit gets away, because if you carry on, if you live long enough, you'll get another chance to capture it, to understand it. And so, when I tell you this story, when I'm standing with Minnie in the kitchen, and she repeats, "Mi hijo, mi hijo," "My son, my son," I'm going to say I threw my arms around her, saying, "Pero regresó." "But he came back."

The Absent Father

My father met the woman who would become his first wife in Fort Polk, Louisiana, in 1954. When I was growing up, he rarely spoke about her. I knew my father had been in the Army and had been married to a woman named Leila, just as I knew he'd once lived in Texas. These topics were bound up with each other. But any questions about them were almost always met with cold silence.

In a photograph, she is petite and shapely, with showy blonde hair and a loose white blouse tucked into khaki pants. Her eyes are small jewels, her cheekbones wide and round, her skin rosy. Her smile radiates happiness.

At some point before I was ten, I became aware of some murkiness in my father's Army history. He'd been dishonorably discharged, but I didn't know why. At most I'd heard murmurings from my parents, picking up a sense of something wrong. It wasn't something we talked about. But decades later, when I was in my thirties, my mother seemed to have had a change of heart. In 2011, after I'd already done much research about my father's life, she shared a folder of records with me. I was surprised by these new documents. Everything I'd written and shared with my mother up to that point had been to honor my father. Now the search was pushing me in an uncomfortable direction.

"I saw this tiny article in the newspaper," my mother said, taking the manila folder from her cabinet and handing it to me. "The military was admitting that many AWOL cases were punished too harshly, and was conducting reviews to reverse many of these judgments."

In the early 1980s, the military began acknowledging many of its members were treated unfairly because of past AWOL convictions made during the "hurly-burly," as my mother put it, of the 1950s and '60s.

I set up my laptop in my mother's living room and began to look over the contents of the folder.

>+••+<

"In the Army, he was 'Joe' and 'Caucasian,' I note with interest," my mother wrote in a letter tucked in the folder. She'd sent this letter to Army officials in 1982, in an appeal to change his discharge status to Honorable. Most unexpectedly, in these records I learned details of the collapse of my father's marriage to Leila because the breakup figured in his 1960 discharge from the Army. Furthermore, an official wrote a narrative of the sundering relationship, a narrative which made its way into his military records.

Before my father received his honorable discharge from the Army, my mother told me, it was hard for him, for example, when applying for jobs or obtaining bank loans. Furthermore, as I later learned, he would have been disqualified from receiving the benefits usually accorded to veterans. He would have been prohibited from ever receiving *any* government benefits, even those based on need. He almost certainly would have been disqualified from government jobs. It's an outcome typically reserved for the most egregious of offenses.

I imagine a scene when Joe and Leila met: The mess hall smells of warm frying grease and faint chemical disinfectant. There's a low hum of an exhaust fan, the rumble of a truck departing outside. A man carries his tray and stands next to a woman at the table.

"I'm Joe."

She lowers her coffee, swallowing.

"Leila." She reaches a delicate hand, wrist bent.

"Leila was a rebel," Aunt Mary told me, prompting Aunt Jeanne's immediate agreement. I was never entirely sure what they meant. Did they believe that Leila was a rebel for starting a relationship across racial and cultural boundaries? Or that she resented authority figures? Or was she, as I imagine, simply brash and forthright (and thus un-womanly) in everyday interactions with my sociable and softspoken Gonzales relatives? In those years, when Joe was in training as an elec-tronics repairman, Leila was working as an air traffic controller, an exacting job that doesn't strike me as an outlet for the family renegade. But it's also a job that in those days was highly unusual for a woman and probably demanded a large degree of assertiveness.

"If we do," Leila says, touching his lips, "we have to get married."

"Will you marry me?" Joe looks at her straight.

"OK. Do you want to spend the night?" she asks. In the kitchen, Joe embraces her, pushing her against the counter. As they kiss, two pans slide from the countertop, clattering to the floor.

Sometime later, Joe awakens in bed next to her. She is still sleeping, her abundant curls like fields of gold on the pillow. When she wakes, she smiles to see him.

The author of his military records wrote, "He knew his wife only three or four weeks before they got married."

According to Aunt Jeanne, Leila and Joe came to the family home on Eighth Street in Austin. They were newlyweds. Andrés offered to let Joe stay in the house; Leila would stay in the apartment behind the house.

The author continued, "When he went to Korea in 1954 his wife remained in the States."

When Leila became pregnant with her first daughter, Miranda, Leila was forced to leave the Army. Miranda was born in December 1955, when Joe was stationed away in Arkansas. Aunt Jeanne said the Army superiors didn't approve of the marriage between Joe and Leila because he was Hispanic and she was blonde and so their superiors stationed them apart. "They made life very hard for them."

In September 1956, Joe, Leila, and their daughter Miranda returned to Austin.

The family car pulls in front of the two-story family home on Eighth Street. Andrés and Minnie come out and greet them warmly on the front lawn. The trees cast rippling shadows over the house.

"Joe," says Andrés, smiling with paternal approval. "Yes, that's it." Andrés picks up Miranda, ten months old, saying, "Ah, such a big girl now."

Leila, Joe, and Miranda lived in the tiny apartment behind the house on Eighth Street for about a year. Joe again took classes at the University of Texas at Austin. He struggled in his return to academic life, and again he would leave the university without a degree. He once again enlisted in the Army. This meant further separation from his wife and family. Over the course of six years, despite the hardships and frequent moves of Army life, they had three children: Miranda, Alexis, and Mark.

When I was growing up, I knew my father abandoned his first wife and their children. I didn't know the circumstances of their breakup. Since he made no effort to contact his wife or these children, I tended to blame him. But with these new details from Aunt Jeanne and Mary, and from the military records, I could acknowledge mitigating factors. Army life took a toll on the marriage of Rene and Leila. As Aunt Jeanne said, the Army *was* set against them. Furthermore, it seemed my father was too young to have had three kids, when he was in his mid-twenties. It was hard for me to imagine a person of that age bearing the responsibility for a family of three young children.

The author of my father's military records wrote, "After Korea, he attended Missile Maintenance School at Fort Bliss. His wife and three children came to Fort Bliss to be with him. He had a friend who was in the same course. He introduced this friend to his wife."

I imagine Leila and this friend are eating sandwiches together in the mess hall, tense conversation passing between them. I picture him with short blond hair, narrow-rimmed glasses. They're both wearing the usual Army fatigues and caps.

"We have to tell him we're going together now," Leila says.

The author of the military records wrote, Joe "reacted violently by tearing up the apartment."

It was 1958. Joe was twenty-three years old.

In the apartment outside Fort Bliss, he throws a vase of flowers against the wall. He flips a coffee table onto its side and kicks the legs until they splinter and break. He rips an Army recruiting poster from the wall. With a knife he slashes the upholstery of the couches and chairs. He pulls the mattress onto the floor and slashes it, too.

Yes, I could imagine my father doing that. It would have been an extreme and rare version of him, but possible.

He was taken to the MPs and kept overnight until he could talk to his commander. His commander told him to hang in there and try to work things out. The author of the military records wrote, "His friend and he were in the top of the course and the commanding officer wanted them to stay in the course."

The children remained with Leila and Joe moved onto the base. When the course ended, both Joe and this friend were assigned to the same school to teach. Joe requested to be assigned to another base because of the circumstances. In 1958, Joe was transferred to serve with a missile battalion at Loring Air Force Base, in Maine.

The author of the military records wrote, "Subsequently, through correspondence with his wife, she indicated she wanted to come back."

>+--+<

In June 1959 Joe drove across the Texas state line in a car towing a trailer.

He'd brought a new table, an upholstered couch, a chair, and a mattress. In the passenger seat of the car, in an open box, was a vase of flowers.

The author of my father's military records wrote that my father drove a car from Maine to El Paso to attempt reconciliation with his wife Leila. Joe had requested and was granted a fifteen-day ordinary leave during which he attempted to meet with Leila in El Paso. His brother Gus told me when I spoke to him in Austin in 2000, "My brother passed through Austin in 1959, saying he was in trouble, he needed money, and he needed help. He was trying to save his marriage with Leila. I gave him some money." Joe also contacted his mother Minnie, who agreed to help him, and she saw her son briefly.

The author of my father's military records wrote, "He had brought a trailer with all the furnishings but when he got to El Paso—"

Joe parks the car and trailer in front of Leila's apartment on a sunny, clear afternoon. He steps out of the hot car, his hair perfectly groomed and his face clean-shaven. Leila with her overflowing curls appears in the doorway of her apartment.

"Will you have me back?" Joe raises the bouquet of flowers.

She shakes her head. Turns; goes inside.

When he returned to his unit, according to the author of his military records, he was very nervous and for several weeks found it difficult to work. "In June 1959, he received fifteen days ordinary leave and three days extension. He departed AWOL from duty 20 July 1959 and surrendered 22 August 1959 which resulted in a Special Court-Martial for the absence without leave." The court-martial sentenced him to six months confinement and reduced his rank to E1, the lowest rank, reserved usually for trainees on their first assignment.

⟩┼╍╸⟨

A single light bulb glows over the kitchen sink where Leila's washing dishes. It's her El Paso kitchen, 1958. She's alone. Her shoulders are hunched, her full blonde hair cascading over them. There's a smell of disinfectant, the linoleum table sticky with grease. I hear a soft whimper, "*hwaw, hwaw, hwaw.*" It sounds like a heartbeat or a distant cough. Where's Joe?

In a letter to my father from the Office of the Adjutant General and the Adjutant General Center of the United States Army dated August 11, 1982, Captain Neal A. Shelley wrote, "I am glad to inform you that, after reviewing the findings and conclusion of the Army Discharge Review Board, the Secretary of the Army directed you to be informed that your discharge has been changed to Honorable. New separation documents have been prepared and are enclosed."

After my father died, when we laid his ashes to rest, an Honor Guard performed a military burial service. Five volunteers, men in their sixties in sharp military uniforms performed the ceremony. At my mother's request I recited in Spanish a prayer to the Virgin of Guadalupe. Church and country were the two institutions that could perform a burial ceremony for my father, and my mother chose country. I remember the three-volley salute, the sharp cracks of the rifles, and the phosphorus smell. I admired the slow ceremony as the men folded the flag. One of the volunteers pressed a paperboard box with the warm, empty shell cases into my hands.

>+--+<

I look like my father. Many people have said it. My grandmother Minnie, my mother, my wife, my cousins. By my early forties, I'd come to resemble my father even more. Apparently I'm the result of some remarkable genetic coincidence with my eyes. They're my father's, or the closest of anyone's.

"Rene," my mother called me, after I'd returned from a long absence. And then: "I'm sorry, I know you're not your father."

My grandmother Minnie: *Te pareces tanto a Jose Rene.* You look so much like Jose Rene.

My cousins: "We used to think Gus's son Joey looked the most like our long-lost Uncle Rene. But now that you've appeared, it's you."

If I were to describe myself in a few words, I'd say I'm a tall, thin, distinguished-looking gentleman with a close-cropped gray beard. I don't refer to myself as "distinguished" to boast. In fact, it's something of a hindrance. Combine this with my somewhat gangly-looking aspect, and my six-foot height, and I tend to stand out in a crowd. The CIA would never employ me to anonymously secrete certain documents out of hostile countries. But closer to home, and more significant to me, as I age, I've become a mirror of my father.

In fact, it's been something of a struggle throughout my life to realize that I'm *not* my father. I don't have to repeat his choices. I'm not guaranteed to suffer his fate.

I spent years talking to people who knew him. His friends wanted to share their memories with me, as if I were a doctor, capable of healing *them*. Maybe one reason my subjects are so willing to speak to me is because of my eyes, as if my father is looking back at them.

But when I look at this evidence from the 1950s, my father seems truly strange and alien to me. When I puzzle over the written account and comments from his relatives, I find myself at a loss, at the greatest distance from him. I know the version found in his military records may not be the most accurate one. It merely seems official because it's from the US government. Nevertheless, I've always had the hardest time with this part of his story, both understanding his alleged actions, and believing the events really happened as they say.

In 1989, a gleaming white Chevy Astro van comes to a stop in front of our Middle Grove house in upstate New York. The van door slides open and three boys tumble out into the sticky August day. They run in different directions, howling at having escaped the tedium of their long car ride. Alexis approaches. I've only spoken to her on the phone before. She's in her thirties, imposing, about five ten, her tight brown curls adorning a squarish face. Her solid and thickset arms and legs make her seem more sturdy than slight. She introduces her sons: Ryan, Matt, and Corby, aged five, seven, and thirteen. They're my nephews, my father's grandchildren. I tell Alexis I'm happy to see her and I look forward to learning more about her and exchanging stories about our father. Alexis says yes, we'll talk. "Come," my mother says, "come inside."

Several weeks earlier, my mother had announced at our kitchen table that Alexis was coming to stay with us. My sister Heather was away at college and I was seventeen, a senior in high school. "She's staying just for one month," my mother said, "While she gets settled in our area."

This was big news. I was curious about Alexis. She had told me on the phone about her friend, the private investigator, who'd helped her find us. The only private investigators I knew were on television, moving in a murky world on the edge of danger. I knew that Alexis had been living in Oklahoma City, a place that sounded like the distant Wild West to me. The townspeople awaited the arrival of their new sheriff with apprehension, and I was one of them. What did she know about my father's past? "She's bringing her three boys," my mother added. "You're going to be the oldest. We're all going to make adjustments to get along."

The afternoon she arrived at our house, the light sifted through the dust as we made our way upstairs. It was an old house with many rooms, ten rooms in fact, three bedrooms upstairs plus a study and a kitchenette and two bedrooms downstairs, and everything was well-worn and had a dated feel.

"There will be plenty of room for you here," my mother said to Alexis, showing her the rooms where she and her boys would be staying.

Alexis smiled. "This is very nice," she said, running her hand along the bedspread.

The youngest boy, Ryan, grasped my leg, upsetting my balance. He had an eager grin. I smiled to Alexis. "He likes to cuddle," I said. She laughed. "He's a sweetheart," she said. "You're his uncle. Uncle Chris." I was seventeen years old and an uncle.

Alexis and her children carried duffel bags and cardboard boxes of their belongings, thumping up the stairs, to the bedrooms. My father entered the front hall, pausing, quietly looking up the stairs after them.

Months ago, my father had spoken to Alexis on the phone. The only thing I remember him telling her was that I was a "gung-ho rock and roller," with seeming pride, referring to the fact that I played bass guitar in a band. I thought of myself as a sensitive, creative type. I was drawn to the wide range of sentiment in rock and roll, but not its rebellion. I wouldn't have described myself as "gung-ho" and was embarrassed by my father's comment.

I was riding in the car with my father. I saw an opening with the impending arrival of his daughter, and I was curious. I asked him what he remembered about his wife Leila and his daughter. He said when he was in the Army he had a crisis of faith and "the only one who stood by me, who stayed with me, was your mom." I knew this story was chronologically askew, placing my mother with him around the time he was in the Army, which didn't make any sense. My mother didn't enter my father's life until eight years after the Army. He said nothing about his first wife Leila or their children. I was nervous about the impending arrival of Alexis, afraid to share my father and his slips of memory and reasoning with a sister I hardly knew.

Autumn turned to winter, and Alexis and her family were still living with us. I was splitting firewood in the snow outside our house when a woman appeared, saying she was with the SPCA. She was concerned because our dog Pepper had outgrown her doghouse in the yard. "Especially if your dog spends the winter *outside*." An accusation. Our dog, a mixed-breed, needed a larger house and a bed of hay. She happened to know of a family that wanted to give away an old doghouse and we could have it if we wanted. I said I'd speak to my mother.

"We could pick up the doghouse in my van," Alexis offered. "The seats fold down. It will fit no problem."

My mother looked at her, flustered.

"The woman from the SPCA said it was a big doghouse," I said. "It even has a skylight."

Alexis drove the van while I sat in the passenger seat, the road taking us through farmland and woods. Alexis said she didn't know there was so much land up here in upstate New York. "When I thought New York, I thought of the city." When I was seventeen I was self-conscious about living where we did, thinking it was somehow backward. We lived in the boonies. I didn't know if Alexis's remark was criticism or praise, but it sounded like praise. She seemed to appreciate the wide-open spaces, the fields, and rolling hills.

We returned home with the doghouse loaded in the back of her van. Alexis opened the rear doors, the huge old doghouse and its Plexiglas skylight consuming the entire storage area. We carefully lifted the hefty doghouse out of the van and carried it to the backyard. We put in a bed of hay. Pepper sniffed, went inside, turning around several times in the coarse hay. She lay down. Alexis and I crouched at the door, peering inside.

"I guess Pepper likes it," Alexis said with satisfaction.

The long nights of winter dragged on. The one-month stay of Alexis and her boys turned into three, four. Alexis found a job in Saratoga working as a paralegal. She and my mother worked out arrangements for sharing the cooking. The oldest boy, Corby, and I took turns carrying out the trash.

Our double family of seven—three adults, two children, and two teenagers—crowded around our dining table: Alexis, my father, my mother, Matt, Ryan, Corby, and me. Spaghetti with meat sauce steamed on our plates.

"I hope y'all like it," Alexis said, lifting her fork.

"It's wonderful, thank you," my mother said, easing forward in her chair.

My father asked Alexis how her job was going. She replied in an upbeat voice that her boss was giving her more hours. My father quietly replied that she couldn't complain about that.

I can't recall much conversation between Dad and Alexis. She called him Dad, didn't she? I can hear her say *my dad*, and "Dad." She adopted him quickly. She searched for her father for nineteen years and she found him. He welcomed her into his home. She stayed for six months. But as much as I remember Alexis and I driving around the countryside to transport an old doghouse, I can't picture my father and Alexis having any sort of conversation while I was present. I can only hear her say, "Dad," to him, and recall that it surprised me that my father was her father too. I always thought of her role as my sister as a little unreal, as if she took to sisterhood more quickly than I was ready to reciprocate. She liked to get things done, and I was too cautious, too quiet, absorbed in school and music. As a teenager, I had issues trusting her, perhaps typical behavior for my age. But my mother and father surely welcomed her during that time.

Alexis and the boys moved out in the spring of 1990, renting an old farmhouse near Schuylerville, a town nineteen miles from Middle Grove. Alexis continued working as a paralegal in Saratoga. My mother had had a conversation with Alexis, letting her know that it was difficult to keep two families comfortable in one house and perhaps it was time to move on. I visited Alexis and the boys in Schuylerville, admiring their two-story, antique-white, nineteenth-century farmhouse on a small plot of land, with plastic outdoor toys scattered in the yard.

The next person to leave our little town was not Alexis. She and her boys stayed in Saratoga County a little longer. The next person to leave was me.

When I graduated from high school in 1990, I needed to distance myself from my ailing father. Oberlin College in Ohio awarded me a financial aid package that paid half my way, and I accepted. The school seemed to me to be far enough away from my parents, but not too far. In my emotional confusion I was ashamed about my father and afraid of becoming like him. I didn't keep in touch with Alexis or her sons.

She moved away from upstate New York sometime in the early 1990s while I was in college, headed back west with her children.

In college, I grappled in fits and starts with my future. I vacillated between a career in neuroscience (to save my father) and a career doing anything else (to forget my father, to run away from his disease). I won an award for a term paper on the etiological processes of Alzheimer's disease: calcium deposits, the tau and beta-amyloid proteins, neurofibrillary tangles and plaques.

In 2000, Jen and I, newlyweds, were living for the year in Mexico City, having made the trip through Texas to get there. I wanted to connect with Alexis again. She'd tracked down our father, found him, *found me*, reuniting us with our family in Austin. It was Alexis who introduced me to the entire Tejano side of my family, brought about my discovery of my Mexican American heritage. My search for my father was also a search for myself and this heritage. The fact that we *both* searched brings us two together. When I started to write about my father, I had no way of finding her.

I sat alone on the Mexico City rooftop patio with my notebooks. The sun was waning. A diesel rig belched, the truck's very weight shaking the pavement. As the sun set, I looked beyond the rooftop wall, over the buildings with their tangles of TV antennas and exposed electrical wiring.

Alexis? Are you out there? Alexis?

As much as I'd hoped that meeting Alexis would shed new light on my father, there was still so much I didn't know, even after she came to live with us. Today, when I look at the life stories of Alexis, her mother Leila, and their families, my biggest impression is that they, sadly, died young. Alexis raised three sturdy, bright boys, working as a trial consultant. She died of cancer in 2020, in her early sixties. Miranda, the daughter of Rene and Leila, herself had two daughters, and was known for taking care of her siblings' children. She loved being a grandma to her three grandchildren. Miranda was known as the family matriarch. She died in 2015, in her late fifties. Their son Mark kept a Facebook profile showing a big, shiny V8 engine under the hood of a classic car, his

'73 Dodge Charger, something he was working on. He had two children and got to know the three oldest of his four grandchildren. He died in 2018, in his late fifties. The three siblings' mother, Leila, spent most of her career working in higher education administration. She became the first woman dean at the University of Texas El Paso in the '80s. She died in 2003, in her late sixties.

Forgive me for telling this story out of order. It would be years before my mother gave me the military records which let me put the details about Rene's first marriage into place, the one that had led to the births of Miranda, Alexis, and Mark. The stories revolve around each other, defying easy determination of origins, of which came first and how the story started. Part of the challenge for me is telling the arc of my father's life alongside the arc of my discovering it. The bottom line: my father was the kind of person who prompted strangers from the past to come forward. Alexis had come into my life, only adding to my sense of mystery about my father. After all, she'd become a detective, locating her father after nineteen years of seeking. If she could find her father, so could I.

The Lover

I'm not the only one searching for connections to the past. This quest of mine is part of a wide cultural phenomenon, greatly speeded by searches on the internet, where people seek lost friends and relatives, children search for their natural parents, and long-separated brothers and sisters are reunited. In February 2000, Jen and I have just made the trip through Texas and down to Mexico City. Along the way, we stop in Austin, where I first learn of Teresa. It's Aunt Jeanne who first mentions her, but she doesn't remember Teresa's full name. She told me the strange story of the time *my father* stopped in Austin with *his* new bride, and she was pregnant, and they were on their way to Mexico. I was astonished. I'd never heard anything about her.

But it's Aunt Mary who shows me the photo from the wedding.

Rene, in his suit and tie, stands at Teresa's side. The pair gathers behind a lace-covered table with the wedding cake atop it. She holds the knife. He puts his hand over hers. Teresa shifts her weight, rumpling her minidress, tilting its rounded collar and square buckle. He is handsome, shaven, with short oil-black curls, happy. She has a broad mouth and quick eyes. They are both smiling, but his expression looks more natural than hers. She looks down at the cake. Two candles burn. A gift bow is taped to the knife. Carnations are draped on the lace tablecloth. In the background, a ceramic decorative plate shows a scene of a humble house in the woods. A built-in cabinet contains a vase, coffee cups, crystal wine glasses, and delicate tea cups. The knife plunges into the cake.

When I'm living in Mexico City, I feel so far removed from this research that I want to be doing in Texas, in upstate New York—in the United States. What can I do, being so far away? It sounds obvious, but a bigger and faster internet makes a huge difference. This culture-changing global network isn't in its earliest days by any means. But there are some differences worth pointing out. From our apartment, I connect using a dialup modem. There are no large social media platforms. When you search for someone's name, there's no onslaught of private companies selling his or her personal data. Not everyone is setting up a personal web page, but many people are. Oddly, this makes the internet seem smaller, more open.

From Mexico City, I make my first contacts with my father's old friends from Ithaca. One of them, Baxter "Kit" Hathaway, tells me about the coffee shop, the place where they used to hang out. And then: "Rene had an affair with a smart, interesting, and dangerous woman named Teresa Sutton," he says, and I'm floored. In the same few weeks of research, another old friend, Tom Hanna, tells me Rene was married to a German artist named Helene and they had a daughter together. I'd never heard about this affair, this marriage, or their daughter. It intrigues me to think I have a secret sister somewhere, and I don't even know her name. I do have the name of her mother, Helene, but no last name. I sit at my computer, reading Kit and Tom's email accounts. The fact that I have an unknown sister begins to sink in. And this affair—who is she? Kit's and Tom's accounts set me in motion, spurring me to conduct further research. The most obvious place to begin is to find Teresa Sutton. At least now, thanks to Kit, I know her full name. And it turns out she isn't very hard to find.

If truth be told, there's nothing particularly clever about my detective work. I'm merely persistent and have a desire to keep seeking. Unlike in a detective story, where much of the drama is rooted in suspense and the timing, in real life progress happens in an uneven rhythm. You stumble around in the desert searching for a drink for weeks, when suddenly there is a downpour. A deluge is the best word to describe what happens next.

In her website photograph, Teresa Sutton is a striking woman of dusk-colored hair with ashen streaks and an assertive smile that conveys a pleasant and firm personality. There's no email address or contact form anywhere on her site, but there's a snail mail address in California. I write her a letter and put it in the postal mail from Mexico City.

>+--+<

I imagine my father standing behind the counter in the frame shop on College Avenue in Ithaca, 1965. He puts a sample of matte board in its folder and then turns to hang a frame sample on the wall. A woman walks in.

"Your letter arrived in my office mail at a moment when I had just returned from a trip to the East Coast, where I spent some time with my son and new daughter-in-law and was musing on history and lost memory. I am very sorry to hear that Rene is suffering from what has to be the most frightening illness of our time, especially for someone who valued his brain as much as he did."

The woman looks around the frame shop. She has rich, long, ebony hair, a wide mouth, and kind, captivating eyes.

"I was twenty years old, restless, bored, and ready to break out of my small-town environment." She was a student at Cornell, a poet and editor of the campus literary magazine, a townie who grew up as the child of a Cornell professor of electrical engineering. She was a member of a minority of Cornell undergraduate women at that time who would admit to being a nonvirgin. Marijuana truly did not appear on campus until a year or two later, when it was everywhere. She was one of twenty-five or so students and faculty who had spent the previous summer in the South doing civil rights work. Protest against the

Vietnam War was a ripple in an otherwise calm pond. She met Rene, she recalled, when she brought a picture to the frame shop where he was working.

"He was handsome," Teresa wrote, "in a distinctly non–Ivy League way: intense, artistic, cynical. He made a pass at me, but only after telling me he was married. I responded. He and his wife were separated, and he'd been living in temporary arrangements with his friends."

Rene and Teresa enter a small kitchen of maple cabinets, walls the color of cornsilk, and vinyl flooring.

"Are you hungry?" Rene asks, holding open the fridge.

"Sure," she shrugs.

The scent of sautéed onion and green pepper fills the apartment.

Later that evening, in the bedroom, the curtains are drawn over darkened windows. Rene's lying in bed, asleep. The apartment is quiet, except for a simmering teapot in the kitchen.

"Rene? Rene?" Teresa calls to him, approaching.

A shrill whistle of the teapot sounds. Someone is shouting in French—is it a neighbor? Rene lifts himself from the bed partway and drops back down onto his back. He resumes gentle sleep.

Teresa unties her cloth belt. Rene lies in bed, his bare chest an opulent saddle-brown, no hair. She slips out of her dress. He sleeps softly. She crawls into bed next to him, pulls the sheet close to her chest. They lie in bed, side by side, her awake, him asleep. She turns to look at him, sleeping there. She caresses his hair, and he stirs slightly. She looks around the room, toward the ceiling, the yellow walls. He awakes halfway and kisses her neck gently. She looks toward the ceiling and touches his hair.

He kisses her neck and then covers her body with his own. She sighs.

"Rene," she says.

When my aunt Mary first showed me the photograph of Rene with Teresa, I was struck by Teresa's beauty and seeming sophistication. Aunt Mary's living room in Austin was filled with collector's dolls. They sat on the living room furniture, gazing at us with their glass eyes. My search was starting to take increasingly strange turns, leading me to hope I could sort things out just by reading people's eyes. My informants would give me these inscrutable looks, like Aunt Mary's dolls. But Aunt Mary was the down-to-earth one of my aunts, an energetic talker with a gritty voice.

"This is Rene and his wife Teresa," Aunt Mary said, passing me the eight-by-ten photo, as if somehow hurt by the memory.

Teresa reminded me of Natalie Wood in the 1960s. Stunning, young, fashionable. Very thoughtful looking, her hair sleek and black, with a pageboy cut, her short dress typical of the time, her skin light. She wore a sleeveless minidress over a light, playful, neutral blouse. There's no sign she's pregnant in the photograph, though both Aunt Jeanne and Aunt Mary attested to that. Rene and Teresa must have told my aunts of her pregnancy. For the record, decades later, it's something Teresa also shared with me.

"I became pregnant," Teresa wrote. "Much to his delight."

Back in Ithaca, Rene and Teresa decided to live together as if they were married. Rene proved to be a supportive partner, frequently attending Sunday meals with Teresa's family. In these gatherings, he was unfailingly respectful of her parents, arriving early or staying late to help them with chores and projects around the house. They were courteous and kind with him. But in private they expressed their doubts: in descending order of seriousness, his age, his lack of academic credentials, his conservative political views, and his shifting accounts about his time served in the Army weren't all they wanted for their only daughter.

I asked Teresa about the trip to Mexico I'd heard about, the time Rene passed through Austin in the 1960s on the way to Mexico.

"I remember little detail from the trip through Austin and to Mexico," Teresa wrote. "I do remember meeting some relatives in a family home."

Andrés and Minnie propose a small gathering of relatives at the house in Austin to celebrate the wedding of Rene and Teresa. Teresa looks around the room—to the clock, the silver tea set, the black lacquer cabinet, the gold crucifix on the wall, to Andrés with his suit and tie, to Minnie in her faded ivory-colored skirts with three ruffles, then to Rene in his funky orange-collared shirt. She feels the weight of her pregnancy. Anticipating these relatives gathering for her, to celebrate her nonexistent wedding, she inhales sharply.

Arrangements are put together, calls made on the telephone. At the appointed time, the relatives arrive—aunts and uncles and brothers and sisters and cousins. The mechanical clock with myriad bells ticks seemingly without end. Someone carries into the room a three-layer cake decorated with elaborate frosting. Family members crowd into the room, amid rising and falling voices. Teresa, wearing the minidress, places herself along the wall, looking about the room with discomfort.

Then, at the appointed moment, with the relatives pressuring her to get in position, she moves to stand at Rene's side. They hold the knife above the cake, his hand over hers. The knife plunges downward.

I remember standing in Aunt Mary's wood-paneled living room in Austin in 2000, a dozen dolls gazing at us with glass eyes, when she passed the wedding photograph to me. It was profoundly mysterious.

But now that I'd found Teresa, not only had the questions multiplied, but so had my doubts about my father's character. He told his own parents that he and Teresa recently were married, when in fact they weren't. He gave the reason for their trip to Mexico to be a little honeymoon, and that wasn't true either. He described Teresa's origins as Russian-Spanish, when the only thing remotely Spanish about her was her name. When I was growing up, we'd heard nothing about Teresa or these travels to Mexico. I had the impression my father needed to invent stories, to conceal his history, as if he believed everyone in a competitive and uncaring world was faking something to get ahead.

Rene and Teresa are riding in the car again, south on I-35 toward San Antonio. It's daylight, blistering, dry, and clear. The morning blue sky contrasts with the reddish-brown landscape dotted with olive green. Grassy prairie gives way to scrub and desert, scattered rocks, cactuses, and spiny bushes. They arrive at the travel gate marking the international border at Laredo. They wait what seems like more than an hour in a long line of cars. Weekend partygoers, vacationers, businessmen, trucks loaded with unmarked cargoes.

"I remember crossing the border into Mexico at Juarez and again at Nuevo Laredo," Teresa wrote.

They pull in front of the cement building with a plate glass window bearing a sign, Palacio de Justicia, Hall of Justice. Rene climbs out of the car, helping Teresa to her feet, and they go inside.

They sign the municipal register in Juarez, Chihuahua, Mexico, and file a petition for divorce in a district court in Juarez. They come out of the building in the early evening.

Teresa didn't say in her letters why they went to Mexico. From her account, I got the impression the trip was just a vacation. Maybe she was repressing or hiding the true purpose of the trip. In any case, she didn't tell me.

When I first learned from Aunt Jeanne in San Antonio in 2000 that Rene had passed through Austin in the 1960s with his pregnant bride, on their way to Mexico, I myself was making the same journey with my new wife. Questions about my father and our family history first planted, then germinated, then sprouted around me. I'd wanted to believe my father was sharing his eagerness for Mexico and his ancestral culture with this mysterious woman. After I put the pieces together, I learned he'd gone to Mexico to petition his wife of four years for divorce. The purpose of his journey to Mexico was alien to me. He was not seeking connections, but breaking them. He had made a sacrilege of what I had come to view as the romance of crossing the border into Mexico.

><+••+><

When I was ten, in my father's room, I rummaged through a drawer filled with junk. Sewing needles, screws, string, a tape measure, buttons, hinges, a broken watch, a length of wound wire, a power supply from a defunct electronic device, three batteries of different sizes and gradations of rust, a calculator tape, dried-out pens, paint tubes, a jar of pennies, an audio speaker without a case, 35mm film containers, masking tape, a short telephone cable, a matchbook from New York City, smooth fragments of beach glass . . .

Among the items that caught my eye was an intricate old car key. The teeth had an elaborate jagged pattern, with complex, tiny grooves on either side of the blade. I was fascinated. On the bow of the key was a logo which read, "Porsche," which I knew was the desirable German sports car. I never heard my father tell a story of owning a Porsche—though he did own some collectible old cars. I didn't ask my father about the key because I wanted to play with it and I was afraid he would be angry that I'd been rummaging in his drawer. I slipped the key into my pocket.

><+••+><

Rene and Teresa covered a lot of ground in a short time, spending just under two years together. In 1966, they left Ithaca and moved to Staten Island. "We shared an apartment where the rent was cheap and we could park our car on the street," Teresa wrote.

"I had a minor production gig for a play that was a precursor to *Hair*," she continued. "I was spending all of my evenings and weekends there and it was a way to be together. Rene helped out a bit on the show as well, and of course his construction skills were much appreciated."

And what about their baby? Teresa had a miscarriage—the baby was a boy.

》•••《

"The relationship began to sour after less than a year in New York," she said. "I made plans to leave but I was afraid to tell him. One day when he was gone I packed a suitcase and moved into an apartment near Columbia, where my brother Jeff was in school."

The breakup of Rene and Teresa hit me hard. I wanted to keep her, to keep seeing her with my father.

After she'd moved out, she came back to the Staten Island apartment once more to gather a few last items. They had a conversation that was distant, bitter, and filled with personal recriminations. She'd lost even a sense of friendship with him. He took off in the Porsche 356 convertible she'd bought from a dentist in Great Neck, New York, because he wanted it so badly. That was the last time she ever saw him. Soon afterward she heard from the police he'd totaled the car.

The road curves—how much has he been drinking? The winding country road shifts and sways. His eyes linger on the gauge cluster behind the steering wheel. His head bobs down, eyes closing, then he snaps to attention. A sharp curve approaches and two trees come up from the side of the road. *Bam.* The car was crushed between two trees.

But I've gotten ahead of myself. When I describe the crash of the Porsche, I'm actually thinking of another car crash, the one in 1984, but we're not at that part of the story yet.

》•••《

Teresa would become an attorney and government official, prominent in Democratic environmental politics and administration. Within a few months of my finding her, she and I would become hesitant friends, going deep, exchanging several letters, each arrival filling in new detail about her impressions of my father and their relationship.

We needed each other after I revealed my father had been suffering the loss of his faculties and was dying. From her stories, I saw his vindictiveness, his bad temper, his volatility. But I also saw reflected in her presence his sharp intellect, his beauty. I needed to learn more about my father, and she needed to revisit some difficult history, to write a new ending and to find closure after their relationship broke apart. I became the one in whom she confided.

I myself confess that when Teresa first came into my life, I still believed my father needed me to save his memory and to rescue him. Later, I knew my uncovering his lost memories wasn't going to stop Alzheimer's from taking him away. But I needed to remember him, if only for myself, to make losing him bearable. My father became one of my charges. I became responsible for him. Once I stepped into that position, I needed to know what it meant to have lived his adventures. I vicariously lived my father's life. I lived through him. At first I wanted to know him when he was full of life. Then, I wanted to live that overflowing life. I desperately wanted to keep Teresa, too, which was why the breakup of their relationship hit me so hard. Shortly after she described the breakup, her emails stopped. Teresa and I had gone full circle. I'd been rejected.

Back when I began my search for Teresa, I'd followed tips from Kit and Tom, my father's friends from Ithaca. A few additional points from my contacts with them bear mentioning here. Tom said that his friendship with Rene went back to the early 1960s, when my father had an art and frame shop in Collegetown in Ithaca. Rene was definitely seen as part of the Ithaca side of the Beat generation. Tom was part of that same scene.

On my mother's suggestion, I'd been reading Richard Fariña's novel, *Been Down So Long It Looks Like Up to Me*, to get a better sense of Ithaca and the wider world in the 1960s. I mentioned to Teresa I was reading it, prompting her to read it again, too. She told me about Fariña's character G. Alonso Oeuf, a portrait, in many ways, she said, of C. Michael Curtis, a Ph.D. candidate at Cornell who left to become an editor at the *Atlantic* and who, Teresa said, served as "a mentor to many literary types." When I was growing up, I knew that my mother, a dedicated writer who also worked a separate full-time job and had raised a family, had exchanged letters and manuscripts with C. Michael Curtis. But I didn't know whether my father was close to Curtis.

Then there was Thomas Pynchon, who was Fariña's friend in Ithaca. I'd spent my twenties reading Pynchon's novels, and my own obsession with Pynchon was profound. Did he know my father? Pynchon himself said, in *Gravity's Rainbow*, "If they can get you asking the wrong questions, they don't have to worry about answers." But he also said, "Every weirdo in the world is on my wavelength." Had I become one of the weirdos, drawn into one of his convoluted plots?

And what about Helene, the woman my father was married to when he began the affair with Teresa? After all these years, Teresa said, she could only remember that she was German, worked at Cornell as an assistant to the famous physics professor Robert Wilson, who later went to Chicago to build an atomic accelerator, and they had a daughter named Gabriela. She suggested I write to the Cornell physics department, where they could at least find her name and some dates.

My next task was laid before me. I was either going to turn a corner where a mystery would unfold, or I was losing my grip on reality. My dilemma was not about searching for lost memory, but a more fundamental problem with the fabric of space-time. How often does one need an answer for which the clue is to contact the Department of Physics at Cornell University?

I did some crazy things. I wrote a letter to Thomas Pynchon in care of his publisher. I wrote a letter to C. Michael Curtis in care of the *Atlantic*. I wrote an email letter to the physics department at Cornell. I told them about my father's illness, asked whether they remembered him, and could they tell me anything about his time in Ithaca.

As I walked to the local post office in Mexico City, carrying my letters, amid the buzz and brawl of city traffic and the cool, springlike air, I was guided by voices. I couldn't tell which voices were my own inspired wishes, which were true and reasonable, and which were the unbalanced imaginings of someone reaching too far.

The only thing clear to me: I was going to have to do some broad searching in order to find the woman known to me only as Helene, no last name, my father's second wife with whom he had lived in Ithaca, of whom I had heard nothing when I was growing up, or her daughter Gabriela, no last name, the child my father had abandoned thirty-six years prior in Ithaca in 1965.

The Deceiver

To Mexicans, the city is simply called Mexico. In the mornings, I'd work, making contacts for my career as a web developer. In the afternoons, I'd write, going over the latest details of my search. But my musings had yet to clarify into anything coherent. I had pages and pages for what I'd begun to think of as a novel.

When I walked the streets near our apartment, I presumed I fit in—dark hair, Spanish eyes, whatever that meant—maybe, except that, given my height, I was a little tall. *Norteño*, people said. But I was not from northern Mexico, where the local men are taller; I was from Middle Grove, 2,600 miles away. A Mexican American living in Mexico City, the trailing spouse of a Fulbright scholar, I was conducting research—about people in upstate New York. I was lucky. This almost-accidental arrangement afforded me time to think and write.

Now, as I drew an outline, certain specifics appeared in my mind. My father's old friends, Kit and Tom, were easing back in the coffee shop for an extended hang session. The silhouette of this mysterious woman, Teresa, would appear and exit. With Kit and Tom's help, I'd established several of the broader strokes: Rene's affair with Teresa. His marriage to Helene, and their daughter. I'd never heard of any of this.

As I came closer to grasping the larger picture, I began to think of my search as a story of two trespasses. One: the affair. Someone had an affair with a woman not his wife. But for me, the first trespass *wasn't* that my father had an affair with a woman not his wife, although he did do that. The problem was that he had a previous marriage to a German artist named Helene Mahler, they had a daughter together, and he kept this marriage and daughter a secret from my mother, Coral Crosman, and our family. I have perhaps a selfish perspective: For me, emotionally, at first, this secret marriage was the trespass that mattered. For his daughter Gabriela, arguably the trespass was abandonment.

The second trespass was my own: after I investigated my father's previous marriage, I revealed his secret. I had my reasons, some of them flimsy: By doing so I could bring his lost daughter into our family. I wished to redeem my father. I wanted people to know the kind of person my father was, and by extension, the kind of person I was. But, as the writer Patricia Hampl would ask, did I have a right to his secrets? No, I had no right. You might believe me if I said I only revealed his secret because I supposed it was a secret *he loved*. But this rings false: if his secret gave him power over the wife and daughter he left behind, and over his new family, I cannot condone this. Therefore, since I had no right to share his secret, my only good reason to break it was that he kept the secret from me.

As fully grown children, at times we find ourselves unable to access or even imagine our parents' private lives. We're so close to our parents, we think we understand them. Yet this secret wasn't a minor nuance of my father's emotional psychology or inner life that I failed to understand as a child. This uncovered milestone once marked a major stretch of road through his personal story. And he buried it as he moved on.

Rene met Helene in Ithaca in 1960. I could picture him working in the early afternoon in the architectural drafting area of Sibley Hall, the main building of the College of Engineering at Cornell University. He would usually begin in the early afternoon, carrying out drafting exercises, and stay late into the night. The drafting area was a narrow room of brick, divided by evenly spaced rows of worktables with modular walls. A central corridor divided the workspaces. One afternoon a blonde woman passed through the room.

Sometime later, Rene walked into the lab and saw Helene. She was twenty-five, with long, straight, blonde hair and high, rounded cheekbones. Her lake-blue eyes gave her an unearthly or ethereal quality. Yet with no makeup, she was ebullient as a young girl.

Born in Dusseldorf, Germany, Helene Mahler had graduated from the College of Fine Arts in Berlin before coming to America. Cornell University needed skilled draftsmen and designers during a time of rapid industrial expansion, and Helene secured one of these jobs, working in the Laboratory of Nuclear Studies.

Moving pictures come to me: Rene pauses in the doorway. Two rows of slate-gray composite countertop span the lab. Helene puts down her pen, gestures to the young man.

"I'm Helene," she says, rising from her chair. He introduces himself and when she asks what brought him here, he says, "Curiosity," shrugging.

I could imagine Helene and Rene, in their Ithaca apartment, 1961, standing at easels, painting canvases. Several of their artworks were propped against the walls. Hers evoked soothing optical illusions, painstakingly detailed. His recalled the work of Robert Rauschenberg, a merger of art and pop culture, combining oil, paper, fabric, newspaper, printed reproductions, and metal. Rene worked before a wood panel, about four feet wide and three feet high. With his brush he touched the red-and-white stripes of an American flag. In the foreground of the painting, overlaying the stripes, a bald eagle raises its wings, about to take flight. Helene, meanwhile, focused on an intimate canvas with detailed patterns of gold, copper, and flax, resembling a mandala with an optical illusion of depth and movement.

My father transported the mandala painting with him to his new life in Middle Grove, keeping it in a closet as he declined into Alzheimer's. Forty years later, his daughter Gabriela, visiting on my mother's invitation, saw the painting and told us that the artist was her mother.

}+••}{

The café was closed in the daytime, and so when I visited in July 2012 I peered in through the windows. I'd come to Collegetown, the neighborhood in Ithaca that serves Cornell University students with low-key restaurants, taverns, and shops, to visit a memory—and a trespass—of my father. It was a short trip across town from my home on a weekend afternoon, but for me it was a special occasion, squeezing in a research trip between work and family obligations.

In my search, I still hadn't been able to uncover the name or the exact location of my father's coffee shop. Still, coming here answered a certain hunger. This was *a* café in Collegetown in Ithaca, and indeed it looked old enough to have been around in the 1960s, or even the 1930s. But it may not have been the actual one. Despite my doubts, I looked through the glass eagerly, holding my hand above my eyes to shield the light.

Wooden posts and beams framed a room of wine-colored floor tile. Tables and benches of different sizes and shapes were scattered haphazardly. People had left carved graffiti letters on the tabletops—heavy etches in thick wood, light scratches in the red laminate. Low, wooden benches enclosed the perimeter.

I imagine, at night, from the inside, the small-pane windows reflecting the electric lights. I see a younger version of my father, remembered from a photograph: glistening black curly hair, eyes like opals, thick arms, an apron stretched over a striped gray shirt. He writes in his notebook, turns away, and walks toward the counter. The scene fades.

}+••}{

Ithaca, 1962. "Where is our relationship heading?" Helene asks Rene. They sit in the living room of their apartment at 212 Cascadilla Street. He says, nonchalantly, leaning back on the sofa, "You know I love you."

"Rene, my second period's late." She touches his arm.

My father bolts upright. "I'll be there for you." He smiles, holding Helene's hand. "Marry me!"

Helene, in a letter dated from this time, wrote to her mother in Germany about how much she loved Rene. "He is my prince," she wrote. Helene wanted her mother to know how significant the relationship had become. Rene himself also wrote a letter to Helene's mother. He had every honest and good intention toward her daughter.

I could imagine my father making reassuring statements to Helene, but I also believed he said dramatic things he wished to be true, but that were in fact hard to make true. Despite Helene's frequent letters from America to Germany to reassure her mother of the stability and strength of her relationship with Rene, Helene concealed the news of her pregnancy from her mother until their daughter Gabriela was born in March 1963. When I learned Helene concealed her pregnancy from her mother, I was inclined to believe that Helene herself didn't fully trust my father's intentions and stability. Yet there was another wrinkle: maybe she was afraid to reveal to her mother that she had met an American man and might not return to Germany.

When I was growing up, my father was simply my protective parent. When I was in my late twenties and began learning about his life, he became a seducer: breaking hearts, leaving, womanizing. A stereotype of a shiftless man. I began to see a kind of beauty in this portrait. He was a strange man unknown to me who was part of a sympathetic couple of lovers. Then a series of lovers. I wanted to see him as someone *not* my father, but a mysterious stranger. I also wanted to see him as me.

〉┼••┼〈

In Ithaca, January 2011, I was sitting in a café with a woman named Barbara Bernstein, in her seventies, with long, dusky, gray-streaked hair tied into a bun. She had big, blue eyes, clear and sharp as day, behind glasses. She had a copy of the *New York Times* on the table. It was cold outside, and our winter coats were bunched up on the backs of our chairs.

"I lived at 212 Cascadilla Street, two houses up on the other side of the street," she said. Helene was already living in Ithaca when Barbara came to the United States. "I came in 1960. Rene came later that year. I got to know him, too."

Barbara and Helene had studied together at the College of Fine Arts in Berlin. "In West Germany in the 1960s, America was culturally dominant in design and art. You had to go to America to live your dreams. Once she arrived in Ithaca, there was the necessity of finding a job. Helene found one in the Laboratory of Nuclear Studies."

Rene came to this laboratory out of curiosity. Helene and Rene fell in love. Barbara moved into her own room in Helene and Rene's house, paid rent, and wasn't involved with them physically or romantically.

She said Rene was not well educated, but he learned a lot through books he read. He could do all kinds of things. He repaired their old, battered car. He bought some plywood and nailed it together and they had bookshelves. Rene had artistic talent. Barbara remembered seeing a drawing of a knee. It was almost abstract, only of the knee. It was very good, but his talent stayed undeveloped. He had no patience or means to sit down and study. He lacked discipline, she said.

I could picture Helene, Barbara, and Rene spreading a blanket, red-and-white checks, on the grass by a pond. It was 1962, midday, sunlit, with clear skies, in a park near Ithaca. Helene opened the picnic basket and began passing out jam and crackers. Then wheat bread, ham, mustard, cheese, and gherkins followed. Barbara poured juice from a bottle into glasses. Buttercups lifted their heads at the edge of the blanket. Rene held one of the flowers beneath Helene's chin. You like butter, he said. She smiled.

Night slowly fell. Rene gathered some twigs, dry sticks, and pine needles, assembling them into a little teepee between some rocks, and set the kindling on fire. As he leaned down, his face near the flames,

Helene pointed her camera at him. A paper-white glow illuminated his face as he was blowing on the fire.

"He was the master of the fire," Barbara said, passing the photograph across the café table. He didn't look so much like my father as like a ghost or a Mexican Day of the Dead mask. "I have three pictures that show your father. Unfortunately, none of them show his full face."

When Gabriela, the child of Helene and Rene, arrived, Barbara remembered her standing in her little bed, Rene feeding her cod liver oil. "She had big, dark eyes as he had. Gabriela had a fantastic resemblance to Rene in her face, and the body of her mother, but smaller."

Barbara remembered some disorder in their otherwise tidy apartment, especially the chaotic pile of junk on the back porch. "It was full of junk, all kinds, mostly metal parts and assemblies, each piece interesting in its own way, but altogether it was a random bunch of stuff, overwhelming, all piled up on shelves and in boxes sitting on the floor, unorganized." Barbara said to Helene, "Together we can sort this, throw things out." Helene was daunted, backed away from that. "I couldn't do it alone. We needed two people. I don't know what happened to that junk collection. Did Rene leave it behind? Cart it to the dump? Of all I have ever seen, that was the most chaotic thing in the whole setup."

"The last thing I remember—" Barbara said. "It happened after Gabriela's birth, about a half year." As she spoke, I imagined the house on Cascadilla Street, its vinyl and maple kitchen.

Rene and another young woman enter the apartment. In the kitchen, Rene opens the refrigerator, takes out some eggs, milk, and a bell pepper.

"Do you like omelets?" Rene asks, holding up the pepper. "I make a mean omelet."

The young woman shrugs and smiles, sure.

He cracks the eggs into a bowl, whisks in milk. With a sharp knife he cuts open the green pepper, smelling sweet, crisp, and tart. Finely slicing an onion, his eyes are tearing. He drops a pat of butter in the pan and turns on the heat. The young woman opens cupboards, look-ing for dishes. A yellow oval shimmers and crackles in the pan. He spoons the slices of green pepper across the center of the egg in a straight line. With the spatula, he folds it over.

"Bring me a plate," he says to the young woman.

She gingerly walks closer with a plate, and he slides the omelet onto it. They cut the omelet in two. They sit in the kitchen, eating the omelet. "It's good," the young woman says. It's late morning. The faint autumn sun comes in through the kitchen windows. The omelet tastes sweet, hearty, and creamy, dotted by bitter greens. The scent of sautéed onion and bell pepper fills the apartment. The air is cool and comfortable.

I could imagine my father enjoying his omelet because my child-hood memories became mixed up with Barbara's story. I remembered my father's fancy, his love of making an omelet. On a Saturday in the late morning around eleven o'clock, carefully preparing an omelet was his favorite activity, in the kitchen in Middle Grove. I still wanted to see my father as nurturing rather than deceitful. I had placed him in a childhood memory to shelter him, to protect myself from the dis-tasteful idea of him as a deceiver, a betrayer. All the same, I had become enchanted with this character I had created of him as a seeker of joy, someone for whom passion was more important than reason and re-sponsibility, for whom love was greater than illness and decline. There was no harm in pretending in a passion that knew no bounds. All was fair. It eased the pain.

Rene and the young woman finish eating their brunch. She stands, pressing the lap of her dress, brushing a few egg crumbs onto the floor, touching his stomach, tracing a line to his chest.

"They left their dishes, went off to the bedroom, closed the door," Barbara said to me in the café. "Rene tried to have affairs with Helene's consent. This attitude toward relationships was in the air, new, going around then. Helene steadfastly pretended the marriage was fine."

"Rene brought one or two women home on separate occasions. They used all my eggs for one of those lunches. No one spoke about it but I felt the tension and unhappiness. There was nothing I could do about it. I didn't want to live in this atmosphere. I wanted out. I told Helene so," Barbara said. "Rene was human, not cold. I could admire his humanity," Barbara said to me in the café. "In any case, I moved out in the spring of 1964, and I never saw him again."

Helene and Rene were so very passionate, Barbara said, it couldn't go on with that intensity. "Once the passion is fulfilled, it dissipates. He needed a new source to fill the emptiness. When Rene left her, Helene was forced to agree to a divorce. I think the woman's name was Teresa."

And so I drew myself a moral map. It was as if my father himself were watching me and speaking to me—long after his illness of memory had silenced him. He said: When it comes to love, stay, sympathize, communicate, talk it over, and work it out. This was the father I came to know, the reconstruction of him that I made. Still, there was one secret I had to shatter, a boundary I had to cross. I had to bring back someone he had left behind. I brought her into our family.

I looked at my watch. It was eight o'clock in the evening, our agreed-upon time. After punching the codes to call long distance from Mexico, I dialed the number given to me by Gabriela, my secret sister, the one I heard nothing about when I was growing up, the daughter of my father and Helene, the wife he'd abandoned thirty-six years ago.

Weeks earlier, I had I received an email. My correspondent wrote, "A professor here in physics remembers Helene Mahler. She had a daughter, Gabriela."

Just that morning I'd gone for a walk in the prosperous San Jose Insurgentes neighborhood near our apartment. A woman beggar walked in the crowd, displaying an open wound on her forearm, a sadness apparent in her humble, limping gait. A pair of schoolgirls in crisp uniforms jumped from a moving city bus. A mother and child stumbled over a jut in the pavement. A helicopter whined and flickered through the sky. Cars and people moved in a relentless march, filled with longing. There was a lightness on the air, the *sequía*, they call it, the drought, a withering greediness, a thirst of air aggressive to living things.

When I heard Gabriela say hello, her voice sounded low and thick, with a Midwest drawl that reminded me of Chicago. As I introduced myself, a sudden jab struck my chest. I was the one who was trying to gather information about my afflicted father, a man who was difficult, but whom I loved. Gabriela and her mother were the ones who'd been betrayed and abandoned by this same man. She talked at a slow, careful pace, with a slight slur. I heard the clinking of glasses and ice cubes. I made an awkward greeting, telling her about the time, eleven years ago, when Alexis first contacted me.

Gabriela said she was an artist; her mother was an artist; her grandmother and grandfather were artists. They were all painters. She was an only child and had been brought up by her mother alone. She felt a lot of anger toward her father who ran out on her, the father she never knew. She had two suitcases he left behind that contained many of his personal effects. One suitcase contained the letters Rene wrote to his first wife, Leila. Gabriela said she wanted me to see the letters. She was two years old when Rene ran out and she had really no memories. She tried to talk to her mother about him, but she was afraid. Everything she learned about him was bad.

"And I had these letters, and I read them, they were about his previous children he ran out on," she said.

I asked if she had grown up with some idea of who her father was, what his story was. She said no. Sometimes she tried to talk to her mother. It was hard to ask her about him. When he left, he was sleeping around. Her mother had to pay off debts he ran up. He got one of those Mexican divorces, and her mother was forced to agree to it.

"When I tried to ask about him, it was always difficult. I tried not to ask," she said.

"What do you remember about your dad?" I asked.

"I have only two memories. I remember him taking me to the barbershop when I was two. And the other memory, around the time they split up," Gabriela said. "They got together for a short while. I saw him when he was working at a bar."

When I was growing up, I knew that my father had left behind a wife and children and I imagined the difficulty they must have known. But I had not known he had left behind *two* wives and their children. My father had become a serial offender. It made no sense to me because he'd been together with my mother for over thirty years.

Yet Gabriela was happy with the life her mother gave her. She had a good childhood with her mother. Gabriela spoke fluent German, and talked to her mother on the phone almost every day. She was curious about her father, but she knew him only through his absence, and stories that portrayed him as a very bad man. She had known a vast emptiness rather than a loving father. She had always thought of herself as German with an unknown Hispanic father.

"I'm glad to hear he settled down with someone," Gabriela said, referring to my mother, whom he'd married thirty-two years prior and with whom he'd stayed. "I hated to think he would go on, running out on other women again."

"You and I are now family," I said to Gabriela, yet it sounded even to me like an ungrounded assertion. I was never going to leave her. But I kept thinking of my father as the cruel one who abandoned Gabriela and her mother. I told her we should take some time to process.

"I could stay on the phone an awfully long time," she said.

"How do you say good night in German?" I asked. "Gute Nacht?"

"Yes. And what is it in Spanish?"

"Buenas noches."

"Yes. Buenas noches."

"Much love."

"Love to you too."

Over several nights and weeks and years of long-distance telephone calls and email letters, Gabriela and I shared emotions, made connections, and assembled a story of our father. Gabriela was smart, down-to-earth, and knowledgeable about art and the art world. An art critic in St. Louis described an exhibition of her work as "rich photographic studies done with good humor, insight, and inventiveness." There was much to like about Gabriela—as a sister, an artist, as a person.

Without knowing the circumstances of Helene and Rene's marriage, the admittedly one-sided story I have pieced together appears to me an example of unconscionable moral failure. My father made promises he couldn't keep. He wanted the passion and fire of romance, but none of the responsibility. He talked about being there for Helene, being her partner in the challenges of raising children and family life, but he didn't back up his talk with action. My father said dramatic things he wished were true, but that in fact required conscientious effort, as well as commitment and time, to make true. He had collapsed in the middle of the narrative of his life, and rather than getting up and brushing off his injuries, acting as a support to those around him, he selfishly retreated inward, lashed out at those around him, and broke off connections with his friends. This behavior seemed dangerous to me because he seemed like such a compassionate person. But when he turned away from you, he could behave ruthlessly, quickly, and brutally. It scared me to think of my father this way, as this cruel person, but this was the truth I'd found, a truth about my father I didn't recognize.

At first, I wanted to save my father. When I realized that I couldn't save him, that he would truly die and I would survive him, I didn't want him to die in vain. I wanted to learn lessons from his life and respond to his difficulties. I said to myself: Go. Uncover secrets. Tell the ones that make you strong. Keep the ones you do not understand until they become clear, maybe forever.

I wish I could say *I would never seduce*, but it would be a tall promise, and it would amount to false piety. To make a claim of righteousness, you have to resist when tempted. I haven't encountered—or sought—such temptation. My problem breaks down into a simple logic: my father kept a secret of a marriage and an affair from us—our—his—new—family. I was horrified (too strong a word?), no, shocked, no, astonished. So it was easy for me to tell his secret, to condemn his affair, to criticize his keeping a secret. I had good reasons for telling. I only wanted to say he was human, good and bad. I brought Gabriela into my life. I wanted the world to know my good father existed. Furthermore, now, I must name a hard truth: I wanted to write, and to understand the world through prose and reflection. My father's secret has been the stuff with which I satisfied my writer's curiosity. Yes, reconstructing his memory has been a source of power and healing to me. Yet, the trespass stands: by telling his secret, I have become an author. I want these words to be my confession. I began writing about my father's life to deal with certain issues I believed I'd inherited from him. To confess my own trespass, I have to reveal my father's. Can I confess someone else's trespass? Do I have a right to his secret?

I could imagine when my father met Helene, he saw an ebullient woman with a heavenly quality, a wave of blush crossing her face. I don't wish to feel repressed by what I learned about my father. Did he *love* this secret? Did I love him more by telling his secret? If my father were still alive, would he would resent my telling? Is this a gift the dead can give? Can you tell their secrets as if they wouldn't hear?

>+→+<

In a photograph, Rene accompanies Gabriela to the merry-go-round in Stewart Park in Ithaca around 1965. The weeping willows border Cayuga Lake in the distance. Ducks dip and snap in the mud along the water's edge.

My father wrote a poem, giving a typed copy of it to Helene, which she later gave to Gabriela. She in turn gave a copy of the poem to me. My father had taken up the subject of the impermanence of memory. But I lost the copy. Some time ago, I can't remember when, I called

Gabriela on the phone in St. Louis to ask if she could make me another one.

"Oh, I'll have to . . . look through his stuff," she said, with hesitation. I sensed the idea of going through our father's suitcases made her tense.

"The next time you visit," she added, "we can look through it together."

But we never did. Increasingly, it looked like my only glimpse into the suitcase from twenty-one years ago would be my last. Apparently, the suitcase was locked in a storage room near her old house in St. Louis, the one she'd moved out of a few years back to take a new job in California. She was unlikely to be able to meet me there. Even if I could speak to the landlord and get the correct keys, there was the complicated question of my independently finding the suitcase among the myriad stored items. What struck me as a risky-seeming research trip began to sound almost impossible.

Gabriela herself seems to focus without comfort on the suitcase. The letters it contains, she says, are between Rene and Leila, and they shift from happy to fraught, until eventually the couple breaks up. I recoil at this, because while the letters may reveal a lot about the emotions of those difficult times, they may not reveal much about the overall arc of Leila and Rene's story. From Gabriela's description, the letters don't seem to promise any new information that would help me see my father in a new light. And I had an adequate amount of negative light.

When I began my search, I truly believed that we as a society should recognize *everyone* who falls victim to Alzheimer's, regardless of his or her faults. I believed a portrait of the sufferer *including* his imperfections would be the most appropriate way to honor him. Such a portrait would leave nothing out that was taken away by the disease. The alternative was silence. I wanted to understand my father: his strengths, his weaknesses, his challenges, his faults. But as the negative stories about Rene mounted, my confidence was being shaken. I had no story. Or at least, no story about a good man lost unfairly to a terrible illness. I just had tragedy after tragedy.

At the end of the year, when Jen and I left Mexico, I left the "novel," too. I stopped working on it, piled all of my papers into a box. The manuscript was like a country I didn't revisit for a long time. I promised myself to one day return to the project, and still carried it with me as a dream. Years later, I would look over the biographies of the main characters in this chapter, scarcely believing how much had changed, how much had stayed the same. Barbara Bernstein, for example, still lives in Ithaca, and still paints some. Helene, for her part, having been employed as an artist and draftsperson, and having raised her daughter while working as Robert R. Wilson's assistant to the director for art and design at the National Accelerator Laboratory (NAL) (now Fermilab FNAL), died in West Chicago, Illinois, in 2015.

In thoughts and conversations about my father, I began to see a different side of him, one apart from the rogue. My father seems to have done more wrong in his younger years, in his twenties and early thirties. By the time he meets my mother, in 1968, at the age of thirty-three, he seems to have softened. Of course, my perspective is biased. My mother is the woman who kept him for over forty years. I was the son who, fortunately for me, had him around. I like to think my mother had this effect on him. They were good for each other. They became better people. He was truly beginning to grow. Or maybe it was *me* that was beginning to grow. I was becoming more forgiving.

The Motivator

In January 1968, Coral Crosman, aged twenty-six, left her home in Schenectady, New York, with a dream of becoming a novelist and took a job as a waitress in the town of Stowe, Vermont. She also earned some money writing a ski column for a Schenectady newspaper, but she spent more of her time at the waitressing job in a cocktail lounge called the Stüberl at Spruce Park, near the base of Mount Mansfield. The Stüberl was one of the few places for miles around where you could get a drink (due to the blue laws in Vermont), and a lively bar culture developed there. She probably crossed paths with Rene in several restaurants and inns along Mountain Road in the winter resort town. But it was at a place called the Shed where they met. He was friends with the owner of the Shed, a restaurant that in those days wasn't much larger than a shack. That January it was very cold, and a good ski report had recently been announced for Stowe.

Throughout my life, I imagined various fictions about how my mother and father met. Outside the Shed, winter snow draped the windowsills. Inside, rough-cut Douglas fir beams and a blazing fireplace made a cozy lodge scene. Rene, a trim figure with black curly hair and lines at the corners of his eyes, watched Coral from across the room. She had ash-blonde hair and high cheekbones, flush from the wine and the cold. Cigarette smoke floated in the air. Rene caught the attention of a waitress, gesturing to the woman with blonde hair. The waitress balanced a glass of sherry on her bar tray as she approached

Coral, set the glass down on her table, and pointed across the room to Rene. He smiled slightly with thoughtful mischievousness. Coral lifted the drink and nodded to the stranger. She signaled to the empty chair beside her. "He looked older than I was," my mother said to me as I sat in her kitchen in August 2009, the year my father died. "But I wasn't that young," she said.

I imagined another, later scene, somewhere else—at the Gull or the Matterhorn—other places my mother talked about. Coral told Rene that she had just finished writing her third novel, as yet unpublished. She said half-jokingly, half-hopefully, "I'm going to sell my novels. I'm going to be famous. All I'll need is for you to take care of my sports car."

This promise appears in my mother's novel, *The First Time for Love*, a serious work with a pulp romance title. The book documents the travails of a worker-writer in an imaginary place similar to upstate New York in the 1970s. My mother wrote the book and self-published it under the pen name E. M. Moses. It was my father who suggested she start her own small literary press to publish her own work when the traditional paths to publishing seemed closed to her. Her book, I believe, closely parallels my parents' lives, and my memories of my parents often get mixed up with memories of the novel's characters and scenes. Yet, this scene is not the first meeting of my mother and father's fictional counterparts. Instead, when the heroine, Samantha Carroll, introduces her significant other, Ramon Sanchez, it happens in a reflection. She is working in a dress shop in Riverdale, a fictitious northern industrial city like Schenectady. *All things change*, my mother wrote. *Ramon had never promised to support her and she said, confidently, it didn't matter; she was strong, she could function.* Ramon soon would become her constant companion.

"Rene was taken aback by how quickly the relationship deepened," my mother said to me as I sat listening in her kitchen. He feared that in his previous relationships he had let people down and that he couldn't provide sustained emotional support. She said they were both reluctant to commit, but time strengthened their relationship.

When my mother told me this story, my father had been living with early-onset Alzheimer's for seventeen years. The disease forced him onto a path of uncontrolled forgetting. Yet even before Alzheimer's, my father had been pathologically forgetting. He'd broken contact with his parents for twenty-five years. His first two marriages ended in divorce, and he no longer communicated with his ex-wives or their four children. These families he'd abandoned were like shadows in the closet that we never talked about. I wasn't sure whether he'd truly forgotten them, or whether he was simply incapable of talking about them. When I began my search, I wanted to honor my father. Instead, I found closets of skeletons, roomfuls of ghosts.

Toward the middle of February 1968, heavy rains came to Stowe. It looked like the ski season in northern Vermont was finished. Coral and Rene discussed whether they should go to Schenectady, or to Austin. The downside of Texas, Rene said, would be to enter that society as a biracial couple. Rene's father had been very critical of him when he was married to Leila, another Anglo woman, and he took a long time to come around and accept her. Rene said in Austin in those days it was not legal for a biracial couple even to rent an apartment together. The antimiscegenation laws of Texas and several states of the southern United States, which had banned interracial marriages, were repealed in the U.S. Supreme Court decision *Loving v. Virginia* on June 12, 1967; however, the atmosphere toward interracial couples, Rene knew, remained hostile. The more attractive option seemed to be Schenectady.

I imagined my parents talking in the ski lodge, seated at the maple table, the coals in the fireplace smoldering. Coral had to stay at her job in Stowe until the ski season finished, but Rene needed a viable place to find work right away. They decided he would leave first, and she would follow later.

"How will you get to Schenectady?" Coral asked Rene, as if doubting it would happen.

"In the Chevy," Rene responded.

"That car has no reverse," she fretted.

Outside his apartment, Rene pushed the car loaded with his belongings down the driveway and into the road. Coral, in the driver's seat, straightened the wheel. She climbed out of the car, brushing her dress down at the thighs. She hugged him, and they said goodbye. He left alone for upstate New York, with the promise that Coral soon would join him.

While forgetting is usually considered a loss, it is possible that we can choose to discard memories that serve no purpose and go about our everyday lives. Remembering in too much detail the lives of our grandparents, previous marriages, and sexual partnerships could impair our present relationships. The scholar Paul Connerton wrote about this topic in his 2008 article "Seven Types of Forgetting." My father may have chosen to discard the families he left behind in order to lead a normal life with his current family. But when I was a child, I thought my father drank to forget us, his current family, too. His slide into Alzheimer's, then, when I was sixteen years old, was the medical culmination of what he had been doing all his life. It gave him a reason to discard all of us—his wife, his daughter, and me—from his mind.

In the spring of 1968, Rene found a job in Schenectady assembling and selling Italian and Spanish motorcycles. When I was a child, my father gave my sister Heather and me black T-shirts with bold letters. One said *Bultaco* and the other said *Moto Guzzi*. The pictures showed cartoon speedsters blazing by on motorcycles.

When Coral returned to Schenectady at the end of the ski season, Rene was living in the room his employer had provided for him, located in a house in Rotterdam near a cemetery where there were no gravestones. The name of the cemetery is now lost to my mother's memory.

We forget by annulment, Connerton says. Our ability to live and act is crushed under the weight of historical scholarship. Information technologies make possible the collection of excessive and unfathomable collections of data, but not memories. Discarding may become as important in the twenty-first century as production was in the nineteenth century. Culling through the junk is more rewarding than passively consuming information. What matters is not the information in the memory itself, but the act of remembering.

In 1971, my parents, with their first child, two-year-old Heather, in tow, rented a house in Clifton Park, then a rural community ten miles from Schenectady. My mother had learned of the house in a newspaper classified ad. The story of how my mother and father found the house is the one told in careful detail in my mother's novel. *House in country, four-bedroom, in need of repair, $90 per month. Samantha read the ad, disbelieving, then read it again. She spoke it aloud to Ramon.*

"Sounds great," he said. "Call."

Ramon pulled up in front of the green house and stepped out onto grass wet with heavy dew. They walked across the lawn to the not unattractive dwelling with its picture window.

This was the house where I spent the first years of my life. I was born in the hospital in Schenectady, but I think of this house as my birthplace. A red, spiral rag rug covered the floor. Soft light came in through the windows. It was a quiet, warm, and peaceful place. But when I was growing up, I had heard stories about broken glass, dust, no running water, and a leaky roof.

My mother was dutifully and obsessively trying—for her art, for literature—to remember every detail of her life even as my father slipped away into Alzheimer's. She had kept a journal and a diary ever since she was a young teenager. As she grew older, she read every day from the Bible and her diary, looking back at entries from five, ten, and fifteen years earlier.

My mother's fictional counterpart, Samantha, gradually gained clarity and self-control during storms in motherhood, work, and married life. It was a good book, but for reasons of length, complexity, and episodic development would face uncertainty in the publishing market. Not very many people read her book. However, I found the book a great consolation, a fascinating testament to a life spent remembering.

To my mother, writing under the pseudonym E. M. Moses, and to her heroine, Samantha, hell is the wreck of a country house—the dream attained, the promise yet unfulfilled, a fetid mess, no running water, a leaky roof, and contractual obligations with the landlady to "fix it up." This Samantha does with the aid of her companion Ramon, as she ventures forth, making necessary repairs. To do so, she must find work to earn money to purchase materials, leading her to a job in a number-obsessed government bureaucracy. This, too, becomes an underworld in her frustrating life, but the money allows her to see, through windows of travel, the sublime—the mountains of Vermont and the seashore of Maine.

Yet my mother's book gives at once an account of significant events in a life and a mundane collection of life's monetary transactions— receipts, check stubs, and payment slips, the amounts all carefully noted. Her pages of accounting weave with subtlety into the narrative or confront the reader as pages of mathematical formulas. In a telling scene, her heroine Samantha and her bureaucratic colleagues are deciding the precise value of one particular student's education. The effect is more disturbing than comical.

She explores themes from a parent's life: baby, childcare, children, marriage, and lovemaking. She conceals a pregnancy to get a job—and keep it—then hands the infant at ten days of age to a caregiver. In my mother's real life, I was that infant.

The sitter gathered the tiny, pink life from Samantha with a gentle eagerness, moving the baby up onto her shoulder.

"Hmmm, he's so light. Just how old is he now?" she asked as they walked toward the front stoop of the sunlit house.

"Ten days," said Samantha softly. In her mind, adding, "Ten days mine—and now the world's."

Samantha has numerical sensitivity: she is able to visualize numbers. Language and numbers are tools to turn pain and loss—those familiar recurrences in life—into power. But Samantha feels regret, loss, and guilt over possessing that power, that is, by taking a job with the numbers-obsessed government. To assuage this guilt, then, she turns to her bohemian lover, Ramon. The dilapidated country house is hellish, yet the family life they have made in it sustains her. There, Ramon, distrustful of institutions, mystically clarifies points of tension for her.

"The salary—do you realize—the salary—$14,000. We can pay our bills and you can retire and paint. We can start all over again!" she projected.

"Hmm," he murmured, "But do you want this job? Do you want to work in a bureaucracy? Will this be good for your writing?"

Ramon, who works with his hands, shows not resentment but skepticism about his "writer" being taken away to the world of work, as if it could be possible to live without work.

Even the netherworld of the ramshackle country house offers moments of comfort. Her children are there; her bohemian artist-husband is there, fixing broken things for her, steadily assisting with the children, until the next rupture. As cobwebbed and dreary as my mother's setting of the country house may be, it sustains Samantha, until the prose is invaded by numbers, money, formulas, and debts.

Beautiful vignettes in the novel ease my mind, such as a quiet moment when Samantha curls up closely to Ramon on their cheap mattress. Scenes of separation and longing between Samantha and Ramon strike me poignantly, because I know my mother traveled frequently for her job. Glimpses of contentment come but are contrasted with a sense of hardship. *Ramon splurged and bought eggnog and a bottle of cheap*

Puerto Rican rum, which they sipped, dusted with nutmeg, before the lit tree on Christmas Eve and, in spite of, or perhaps in triumph over the previous days' tension and anxiety, she felt warm and happy.

Ramon is a mild-mannered, easygoing drinker, mechanically inclined, mystical yet grounded. He was constant and stable; bohemian, but not shiftless; dedicated. I began to admire Ramon more than my own father because he seemed permanent as a rock. I suppose my mother needed to sustain this fiction of my father. The illusion worked for me as much as I presume it did for her. My mother had taken on the responsibility of remembering for both of them. My father and his memory would not return, but I found solace in the pages of her sprawling novel.

My mother, who had claimed to be reluctant to commit to my father, stayed with him for forty-one years, despite his alcoholism and, later, Alzheimer's. When I was young, he could be a bitter, hard drinker, and impressions of his alcoholism rippled throughout my life. But when I asked my mother how she and my father had stayed together for so long, she said, "I wouldn't let him go." When I was a teenager, I remember her thanking him for being stable and telling him that he was her harbor. By repeating her wishes, she made them true.

If my mother's version of my father is bedrock, a grounded and steady supporter of our family, my version of him is a gorge stream. The flow is magnificent, dropping dramatically, dangerous, with beautiful, deep pools and strong currents, filled with debris of fallen trees and rocks, with holes in the bedrock below. Water rushes over hidden holes, creating eddies that can't be seen, with powerful currents that can trap even the skilled swimmer.

>∻⊷⊰⟨

As Connerton wrote, in kinship societies of Southeast Asia—Borneo, Bali, Philippines, rural Java—families remember siblings and cousins, not ancestors, and not dead parents. In these cultures, memory is horizontal rather than vertical. Connerton argued that when consumer capitalism prevails over the past and future, there is less stability for contemporary subjects. Without memory, we cannot judge or critically engage our world. We are powerless against governments and corporations that tell us what to remember and what to forget. Thus, we talk more of identity—our jobs, our roles in the system—and less of memory, how we came to this place. We forget in humiliated silence. In order to survive, we bury memory beneath the reach of expression.

>+++<

There comes a turning point in *The First Time for Love* where we say goodbye to Ramon. He doesn't exit the novel in a scene, such as getting into a car alone and driving away; rather, he fades away in a reflection of Samantha's.

To read on one must care more about her and less about the shadow of Ramon, blessed anchor that he is, more about the intense solitude of her interests than the two bright, clever, healthy Sanchez children she and Ramon are endeavoring to raise. Calm and steady, Ramon took care of his family, not straying, supporting his wife and children when they needed him.

My mother had selectively remembered my father in this loveable Ramon. Yet I couldn't reject this good-natured version of him because it would hurt too much. Furthermore, I don't think she deliberately created a harmless version of him, denying how difficult he really was. No, she created the more virtuous man that she wanted him to be in real life.

Ramon returns in a scene at the very end of my mother's novel. As I pieced together stories about my father—trying to get at my version of him—I memorized his last words in the novel. I relished them.

In Ramon's last scene where he speaks, he climbs into a car with Samantha. She has just finished running a marathon in the Adirondacks. The year was probably 1979. A song comes on the radio, and Samantha realizes that for several years she has been trying to recall the name of the artist. The announcer says the name of the band is Cream.

"That's your group," Ramon said quietly: *"the one you've been trying to remember."*

Those were Ramon's last words in *The First Time for Love*. The recollection of the name of the band stands for the pleasant return of memory about a life, about the past. These words played on my mind, turning over and over. I placed them in and out of the text of my own book, as their meaning began to transmute. "The group" transformed in my mind to the people—the friends, lovers, acquaintances, parents, brothers, and sisters my father once knew but forgot after he became ill, all the ones I assembled, consulted, sparked into reminiscing, and mined for memories, all the people in whose shoes—and from various vantage points—I had repeatedly imagined myself. "That's your group," my father said quietly to me: "The one you've been trying to remember." He breathed in a labored, bullfrog groan. His loved ones gathered around him on his deathbed.

>+++<

I learned from both my mother and father some truths about remembering and forgetting. From my father I learned that sometimes we must discard memories in order to go about our everyday lives and protect our present relationships. You may love someone who is difficult, but forgiving his wrongs begins with forgetting. And no matter how many people we ask, no one but you will ever understand the decisions you make about love.

From my mother I learned that writing and remembering give you discipline, clarity, and self-control in the storms that come in life. You can create in your mind the strong and reliable person you want your loved one to become, and it will help you brace and support him. If you repeat how much you love him and tell him that you won't let him go, it will help him become resilient.

I learned on my own that remembering is a process. I spent thirteen years listening to my father's old friends—in kitchens, in letters, in emails, on the telephone—as they talked about their memories of him. They were eager to speak to me, as if ordinary aging were a kind of illness of memory, and I was a therapist helping them heal, pulling memories into life. I loved listening. Their recollections enriched my understanding of my father far beyond what I could have done on my own.

And I learned from Connerton that without memories, we become useful for armies and corrupt bureaucracies, amoral and powerless against them. He has a point, too.

As I write, I am *remembering* how my mother and father came together. This is a simple story. Two lovers met in Stowe, Vermont. Coral was twenty-six, Rene was thirty-three. They returned to Schenectady, New York, and later moved to a country house in Clifton Park. After I was born, I came home to that place. My mother wrote a novel in which she spent a lot of time keeping track of numbers—all the accounting, so much accounting. After working for the New York State Education Department, Bureau of English and Reading Education, for four decades, and self-publishing six novels and five books of poetry, she herself began sliding into Alzheimer's at age seventy-nine, and moved into an assisted living facility. The thief would assail both parents.

In the Adirondacks in 1979, I was standing beside the road in the shade with my father and sister, waiting and watching the runners go by, with their bright clothing and legs wet with sweat. Trees swayed in the cool breeze. I was seven years old. I heard the cheering crowd, my ears popping in the heat. I drank water from one cup, holding another. My mother, who was thirty-seven at the time, appeared, running toward us. "Way to go," my father shouted, and my sister and I brought cups of water toward her.

After the race, my sister and I got in the back seat of the car and my mother and father climbed in the front. My mother said something to my father as he started the car. On the radio, a loud, distorted guitar was riffing. My father turned to my mother and spoke, very softly, very quietly, but I couldn't really hear what he said. The drums and the bass kicked along. A singer partly yelled, partly sang something I couldn't understand. My mother spoke hurriedly, and my father turned to her and smiled. And I remember this, with a little help from my mother and father.

The band playing on the radio was Cream.

The Fictional Character

My mother used to say something interesting about my father: he always claimed that the Hispanic character in Richard Fariña's novel *Been Down So Long It Looks Like Up to Me* was based on him. When I was in my late twenties and hearing the story for the first time, the mere possibility that it was true bowled me over.

Richard Fariña's comic novel of growing into adulthood was viewed in certain circles as one of the great American counterculture novels of the 1960s. If my father actually inspired a minor character in the book, it would be an earth-shattering connection. Only one degree of separation would loom between me and greatness. Huge crowds of now–middle-aged boomers would sweep in, lift me up, and carry me through the streets of my town, invincible. Finally, I would gain some unblemished clarity about my father. I would look around at the spiffy buildings of our town, and at the cheering people waving, finally understanding him, and myself.

I was the one who, at the time, had collected numerous pages of notes about my father, hoping they would resolve themselves into my first novel. As the threads of my father's memory unraveled, I was painstakingly re-creating him as a fictional character. But if he truly inspired *Been Down So Long*, as he claimed, Fariña had previously done it—to astounding success. It would be ironic, because I had so struggled with the idea of my father as a failure. Little did I know that Fariña had already recognized my father's magnitude. I started to develop a quiet hunger, wanting the book to provide insights into my father's personality. What was he like in those days? Was he a partier? Was he already doing crossword puzzles? What did he dress like? How did he wear his hair? Pretty soon I was drifting off into the imaginary.

There, my fascination grew to sizable dimensions. Thomas Pynchon, who was friends with Fariña in Ithaca, stood alone as my absolute favorite author. "A screaming comes across the sky." "Everyone's equal. Same chances of getting hit. Equal in the eyes of the rocket." *Gravity's Rainbow, V,* and *The Crying of Lot 49.* I loved all of them. I learned of Pynchon's friendship with Fariña when reading the introduction to Fariña's book. This was years before I lived in Ithaca—then, it merely was a charming college town in upstate New York I had visited with my family for my mother's marathons. Pynchon, famously, was a reclusive, privacy-craving author—never giving interviews to the press at all. His work itself was monumental; his novels and essays were his only communication to the outside world. If I could somehow prove this connection to Fariña, perhaps I could break through the veil of secrecy and get closer to my favorite author. Lastly, I'll name an additional—perhaps selfish—point. Such a connection between Fariña and my father would be a *fabulous* thing to write about.

Wading deeper into the waters of my "novel," I started to talk about it with writers of a certain generation in my town who had read Fariña when the book first came out. "That's fascinating!" one said. "Oh my god!" one woman remarked. "I can't believe it! Tell me more!" A third: "You filthy dog! Found yourself quite the bone!" My spirits buoyed, I returned to my mother, pressing her for more details. But she seemed downcast, as though recalling my father's younger days stirred great emotion.

"At one time," my mother said, "your father attracted people with his magnetic personality. You, Chris, never did get to know him the way he truly was: sensitive, brilliant, artistic." He loved to dress up, go to parties, and had an active social life. He enjoyed all that. "But," she said, "he ended up losing all of his friends."

My father may have mentioned Fariña at some point in my adolescence, but I barely knew who Fariña was. My father had become ill just when I would have begun asking him questions about his own coming of age, his own youthful rebellion. I was curious about Richard Fariña, but I couldn't speak to him directly. He died in a motorcycle accident on April 30, 1966, two days after the book *Been Down So Long* was published. He was twenty-nine years old.

Fariña's book, set variously at an upstate New York university, in the American West, and in Cuba, traces Fariña's experiences of a campus in revolt, interwoven with a growing awareness of the human cost of war in Vietnam, the suggested freedom in jazz music, the progression toward revolution in Cuba, and violence, witnessed in the detonation of an atomic bomb in Nevada. The main character, Gnossos Pappado-poulis, grapples with his own mortality as his delusion of being exempt from death gradually fades. Pynchon wrote of *Been Down So Long* that it "comes on like the Hallelujah Chorus done by 200 kazoo players with perfect pitch," and dedicated his 1973 novel *Gravity's Rainbow* to Fariña. The book is considered a celebration of the youth counterculture of the 1960s. Millions of copies were sold.

The Hispanic character in the book is named Juan Carlos Rosenbloom. Yet in my first reading of *Been Down So Long*, despite my fascination with Fariña, it seemed impossible that this Rosenbloom bore any resemblance to my father: *"My name is Juan Carlos Rosenbloom," said the one in a sequined rodeo shirt. "From Maracaibo." He strained formally over the red plastic tabletop, stretching out a minuscule, hairy hand.*

My heart sank. *"Not more than five feet tall,"* Fariña wrote, *"Saint Christopher medal tight on his throat, grease mat for a head."* The scene fell apart. Juan Carlos Rosenbloom didn't look anything like my father.

Why would my father claim to be this lousy character? He had deceived my mother and me. I'd approached my reading of Fariña's book with a certain degree of solemnity, hoping I could write something significant and illuminating from what I'd learned. But already I could hear Eleanora Foss from the third grade cursing my father as a scumbag, this worst of all possible insults, after I'd mentioned that he worked at the video arcade at the mall.

Certainly, the resonance of the names Juan Carlos Rosenbloom and Jose Rene Gonzales suggests a relationship. I wanted to see my father in Juan Carlos, especially when he plays the role of the tough, loving friend to Gnossos. In the climax of *Been Down So Long*, the night before Gnossos departs on a boat to Cuba with companions Drew Youngblood and Juan Carlos Rosenbloom, on a mission to participate in revolutionary activities, Gnossos, in despair over love and other existential problems, sitting on the docks above the water, flirts with throwing himself into the sea, and it is Rosenbloom, racing to his aid "*like Speedy Gonzales*," as Fariña put it, who wrestled with him, finally restraining him. I wanted to possess that character, that strong friend, for myself, for my father.

But I never heard my father tell a story of visiting Cuba. According to my mother, my father once said Fariña based the novel's character on him, but at other moments he said it was a composite character: one part himself, one part another person. Perhaps he and Rosenbloom would turn out to be interesting standins, counterparts to each other. Maybe they had been friends. Maybe I could learn more about what happened on these travels in Latin America if I found the other part of Juan Carlos Rosenbloom.

My heart wanted to believe that my father was an inspiration for Juan Carlos Rosenbloom. I became delusional, even self-mythologizing, like my father. If he was Rosenbloom, then I was Gnossos. Time was knotted together as a single thread, and it would flow through us, and we would both proclaim our exemption from erasure.

When you're twenty-eight years old, and you encounter someone in a story who might help you learn about your father, you can do two things: you can run away, or you can make him your friend. I decided to make Juan Carlos Rosenbloom my friend. If he could save Gnossos from throwing himself into the sea, then surely he could help me save my father.

Kit Hathaway recalled my father working in a coffeehouse on Eddy Street where Fariña used to play. He also said my father worked late nights in the School of Architecture drafting area in Sibley Hall, the principal building of the College of Engineering. According to biographer David Hajdu, Fariña had enrolled at Cornell to study in the intensely competitive engineering program before transferring to the creative writing program. Kit said, "Actually, it's quite likely that your father hung out with Fariña." Kit would sometimes go to the Collegetown parties of the bohemian set and Rene was usually there. Pynchon wrote in his introduction to the Penguin Classics edition of *Been Down So Long*, "It happened that in '58 and '59 there were a number of students from Latin America in the School of Architecture, and their circle was one of several that Fariña could move in with some intimacy and ease. Their weekend parties were regarded as the best around." Pynchon and Fariña "hung out some, at parties, at beer outlets on campus like the Ivy Room, or at Johnny's Big Red Grill (called Guido's in the book), which was the usual nighttime gathering place." My mother confirmed that my father knew C. Michael Curtis, a contemporary of Fariña and longtime fiction editor of the *Atlantic Monthly*, and who, according to Kit, Teresa, and Hajdu, inspired the character G. Alonso Oeuf in *Been Down So Long*. Certainly enough, my father shared with Fariña some of the same settings and hangouts around Cornell University, and a few acquaintances.

However, after spending some time getting to know Rosenbloom, a few pieces of the puzzle simply don't fit. There's a scene in *Been Down So Long*, at a party, where some characters are talking about Rosenbloom's origins. How did he get the name Rosenbloom? It's revealed that he was German and Jewish. His parents sent him to Venezuela, afraid the war would spread, and had him converted to Catholicism. Throughout the book, his devout Catholicism is represented by his clutching a St. Christopher medallion around his neck. As far as I know, my father, although brought up in the Catholic Church, was neither Jewish nor a practicing Catholic, and would never wear a medallion.

Furthermore, I had difficulty in locating my father in Ithaca at the time of Fariña's undergraduate years, which, according to Hajdu, concluded after the spring term of 1959. When I spoke to Tom Hanna in 2012, he said he himself arrived at Cornell in 1959, after Dick Farina (as he was then known, without the ñ) had left. I had Army records showing my father was transferred to Loring Air Force Base on April 2, 1959. I hadn't traced him to Ithaca in 1957–59, Fariña's undergraduate years, the time I believe inspired much of Fariña's writing about his college experiences, corresponding to the sections of the novel where Rosenbloom is omnipresent. Yet it was still possible, given that Fariña worked on the novel for five years before publishing it in 1966, returning to Ithaca many times on the folk music circuit.

Meanwhile, Pynchon, writing in the introduction to *Been Down So Long*, had dismissed any attempt to identify who inspired the characters. "There isn't much point in naming names here," he wrote. "They know who they all are and they walk among us, even today."

The reclusive Pynchon did not respond to my letter sent in care of his publisher.

>+--+<

I stood in the sunlit dining room of our Saratoga apartment, where my wife and I, recently married, had moved from Mexico City, holding an unopened letter from C. Michael Curtis. It was the summer of 2001, afternoon. Jen came to my side. Curtis, one of Fariña's roommates in college, was a man of incredible energy who, according to Hajdu, held numerous influential positions as editor of the school literary magazine, editor of the humor magazine, coeditor of the yearbook, and editorial writer for the *Cornell Daily Sun*. I thought of C. Michael Curtis as the longtime fiction editor at the *Atlantic* who had been sending polite rejection letters to the submissions of my mother over the years. In our Saratoga apartment, I held in my hands a response to the letter I had sent. With a nervous hand, I opened the letter and carefully removed its contents, small sheets of *Atlantic* stationery with a message composed on a manual typewriter.

RETURN OF THE LOST SON

"I am sorry to hear of your father's illness," Curtis wrote.

I do remember your father on the Cornell campus and around Ithaca.
He had a relationship with a woman named Teresa Sutton. I don't remember your father in Fariña's circle, though it may have happened.
As to the person who inspired the character Juan Carlos Rosenbloom,
I have always assumed this character was modeled, at least in part, after Juan Felipe Goldstein, a student who was a contemporary of Fariña
and me. I do remember your father as the husband of Coral Crosman,
the writer, and they always seemed happy together, although I'm sure
Alzheimer's wasn't any picnic. With kind regards, C. Michael Curtis.

In the sunlit living room of our Saratoga apartment, Jen did not
miss a beat. She said, "You're just going to have to track down Juan
Felipe Goldstein."

〉〉●●✦〈

I found someone named Juan Felipe Goldstein and called him on the
telephone. When a man answered, I thought, here I go with my crazy
story, talking to a complete stranger about my father with Alzheimer's
who lived in Ithaca in the 1960s, ran a coffee shop where Richard Fariña
used to play. My father, immortalized in a classic novel many people
believed to be one of the great countercultural novels of the 1960s.
Gnossos and his attempted suicide. Juan Carlos Rosenbloom racing
to his rescue *like Speedy Gonzales*.

All of this came rushing to mind. But when the man answered, I
simply asked, "Is this the same Juan Felipe Goldstein who studied at
Cornell in the late 1950s?"

No, he said. That was his father. This was his son, also named Juan
Felipe Goldstein. I cleared my throat. Was it possible to speak with his
father? Was he there?

"I'm sorry," he said. "My father died of cancer several years ago."
His answer hit me like a punch in the chest. Yet I was speaking on

the phone with the son of the real Juan Carlos Rosenbloom who I imagined was out there somewhere. I had found him. What was his story?

He said his father studied at the School of Engineering and graduated from Cornell in the late 1950s. He never knew his father well. His parents were separated. He was raised by his mother in Colombia and had only recently come to the United States to pursue an MBA at the University of California at Los Angeles. His father was rather distant and he would have liked to have known him better.

I realized then that I was searching for a person who knew my father, but instead I found another son who had lost his father.

Juan Felipe said he felt ashamed that he did not know his father better. It was too bad, he said, because his father had an interesting background.

"Sent to Venezuela as a child during the Second World War?" I asked hopefully, recalling what Fariña had written about Rosenbloom.

"No, Colombia," he said, "But yes, during the Second World War."

"Juan Felipe," I said, "I believe your father inspired the Hispanic character in the landmark novel of the 1960s *Been Down So Long It Looks Like Up to Me*."

"You say he is a character in a famous book?" Juan Felipe's voice cracked with astonishment. "I've never heard about it. What is the book? What is it about? This is the strangest phone call I've ever received."

Juan Felipe was perceptibly stunned. We talked a long time. I told him all about Fariña and *Been Down So Long*. He said he would go out and buy the book right away.

>+••+<

I know my father admired Fariña. I believe he was a casual acquaintance of his in Ithaca, though I have no evidence of this other than my parents' anecdotes and the surmises of my father's friends. Nevertheless, reading Fariña gave me a glimpse into my father's world. It is a small comfort to imagine my father reading Fariña, laughing with him, turning each page with pleasure. More than this, I will say without hesitation that I am the one who gave the gift of Fariña to Juan Felipe Goldstein's son. Finding this one true son has been one of my life's proudest accomplishments.

But what about the initial question that spurred me on my search? Did my father inspire an important countercultural novel? I hesitate to speak candidly because, as a son, I'm expected to maintain a certain decorum regarding these family myths. My two voices—the son and the writer—are in conflict right now. As the son, I'm protecting my father, shielding him from the writer, the one who exposes, who trespasses. But it must be said. I don't believe my father inspired Juan Carlos Rosenbloom to any meaningful degree. When I say this, I can hear Eleanora Foss: "Scumbag!" I insist, no, he was a good man. He was loved. It makes sense to me that Rene was a casual acquaintance of Fariña's, indeed admired him, but took it to the level of fantasy to say he inspired a character in the novel, if only to convince other people to read the book.

Even as my father reached his late sixties, after he'd been beset by Alzheimer's for twelve years, people were still calling my mother to ask about him, asking *me* how he was doing with heartfelt concern, or coming to see him. I'm convinced it really changed me, made me more understanding of him. It no longer mattered that he wasn't the real Rosenbloom. The two streams were going to merge into the same pool. My father's fragments of memory that defined him, constituted him, that I'd been gathering, began to collect in my vessel. Still more I carried in my hands. I'd hold this tiny shard on my fingertip, a fleck so small you had to hold it a certain way so it wouldn't cut. This was how you prevented someone from being erased. But ultimately I knew he would still die and I would survive him. The story wouldn't help him. But it would help us, as we merged into one.

The Bohemian

A large painting used to hang in the living room of my childhood home. I think of it as the one with the dark-blue letters over a murky orange background. A wisp of a figure, perhaps a foot high, squeezes between two of the letters, as if having been exploring the stacks in a library, and now, burdened by the weight of all the words, pauses, mouth open with melancholy. At some point in my youth, I became aware that the artist of this painting was my father.

The first time I heard my mother call my father a bohemian, I wasn't sure what she meant, in the way a child might not fully understand a political abstraction like "conservative." Early on, as I began to notice her repetitions of the phrase, I didn't understand my father as a bohemian, whatever that was, never mind recognize his choice of lifestyle on the fringes as his antidote to the monotony of middle-class professional routine. Later in my life, to help me tease out a clearer understanding of my mother's phrase, my wife suggested I read Elizabeth Wilson's *Bohemians: The Glamorous Outcasts*.

Wilson writes that the bohemian idea is closely connected to the art market. With industrialization in the late 1700s, market relations grew up alongside old systems of artistic patronage. Where before artists had been commissioned or given pensions by patrons and the academy, they now could sell their artworks directly to buyers in the art market. This transformation meant the artists were liberated from aristocratic patrons and their biases, only to become dependent on the growing middle-class culture and its tastes. Certainly, the market wasn't friendly to every aspirant. Artists cultivated the idea that, if the artist didn't succeed, it was the fault of society, not the artist. Pushed to an extreme, to succeed was to fail and vice versa. It also meant that admitting failure, on capitalism's terms, became heroic.

As a child, I gathered many disapproving impressions of my father. He kept a collection of his own paintings and drawings, but no longer painted or made drawings. He took artistic photos but never published. He subsisted on a variety of low-paying jobs with minimal responsibility. He took some college courses but never completed a degree. He often drank to excess, until, when I was twelve, in a remarkable transformation, he joined Alcoholics Anonymous and proudly talked about it with everyone. As I've matured, and gotten to know my father better, I've come to realize he was a person unlike anyone else, not any given "type." But even so, the bohemian myth explains so many things about him and the world.

Ithaca, New York—this city on the southern shore of Cayuga Lake, with its landscape of waterfalls and gorges, and fertile ground of lefty politics—surely was Rene's introduction to bohemia. The city broadcasts its penchant for the arts, and magnifies all things related to outsider culture. Its reputation as a progressive hub continues to this day. When Rene arrived here for the first time in 1960, for him the Northeast stood for unprecedented freedom. Just out of the Army, he'd come to study architecture at Cornell University. It was Helene who led him into Ithaca's art scene; she may have even given him introductory painting lessons. A mutual friend recalled her preparing canvases that would appear in a regional show in Utica, New York. Their daughter, Gabriela, said her mother exhibited work at a local establishment called the Upstairs Gallery. Rene, for his part, struggled in the competitive architecture program and eventually left without a degree.

Soon Rene was running a coffee shop on Eddy Street—the one where Richard Fariña used to play. Tom Paxton. Peter, Paul, and Mary. Other folk singers also performed there. I picture Rene waiting on tables, wearing a white apron, taking orders in his notebook, and encouraging customers to read their poetry or display their art there. I never did identify the precise coffee shop, but his friends all remembered it and talked about it. They also used to hang out and drink at a bar called the Palms. Rene made runs by car to New York City to buy bagels for the coffee shop, then about a five-hour drive on a two-lane road that was considered something of a lifeline for Ithacans and formed a fluid connection between Ithaca and the city.

I don't know when my father started making art, but I believe Helene inspired him to make art in a more serious way. I also believe the orange painting with the dark-blue letters comes from this period. When my father changed his name to Rene—and I presume it was around this time that he did—it was a choice that to my English-speaking ear sounds more French, or, shall we say, bohème. As he moved deeper into bohemia, he made this seemingly ethnic shift: from Mexican *Jose*, to Anglo *Joe*, to international bohemian *Rene*. I've often paused at great length over this change, because it seems to say so much. I believe my father was making the most of an exotic image people had of him.

The term "bohemian" in France traditionally had referred to the Roma, thought to have come from Bohemia in central Europe. Together with the Wandering Jew, the bohemian was often racialized as a dark-skinned "other": they were outsiders, perhaps even criminals. Their choice of a life on the margins—and their racial and class ambiguity—was seen to be a political and social statement. I remember my mother saying once, in hushed tones, that my father might be a gypsy. She didn't mean the historic, real-world Roma peoples. Nor was it used as a slur. Rather, my father's bohemian character, like the one in her novel—her romantic gypsy, as imagined via one of her favorite poets, Federico García Lorca—was a lifeline. In her mind—and soon, mine as well—the outsiders could spontaneously become saviors and heroes. By refusing to be conventional, you, as a bohemian, assert your independence from a brutal system. The myth allows us—all of us in society, not just participants in bohemia—to function, despite capitalism's fault lines.

When I was about eight years old, bicycle thieves helped themselves to my father's and my bikes from our garage. My friend Jimmy and I walked the neighborhood, asking, we thought, in an innocent way, whether anyone had seen our bikes. One family, or pair of families, with teenagers a few houses down, beyond the crick and the swamp, took offense to our questions, believing we were accusing them of the theft.

At first, they came at night. We were sitting watching TV in our living room when an object crashed through our side window. It turned out to be a large glass marble. In the weeks that followed, they came in broad daylight, as if emboldened. Three young men rode by our house, doubling up on two bicycles, and with a slingshot broke another one of our windows—a side window that happened to be next to a large picture window. We *saw* them do it. In the subsequent days, they rode in menacing circles in front of our house. My father finally had enough and went out to confront them.

"We'd like you to pay for these windows! We saw you do it. End this nonsense now!"

"Don't give me the evil eye," one of the teenagers shouted back. "That's harassing me! You have no proof! I got three men in jail for harassing me!"

This went on, it seemed, for the whole summer. They came back with a pellet gun—an air-powered rifle—shooting from a car, a green AMC Gremlin, and hit the picture window, but it didn't shatter. The boys returned day after day, putting more pellets into the picture window, until four or five spider webs spread through the window, but it didn't collapse. The metal projectiles may as well have been lightning bolts. For weeks, a throbbing electric current of terror coursed through me, but my parents acted as though the assault were a mere nuisance. They may have been scared, but they didn't let on. They called the police several times. They called our insurance. The window was replaced. My parents lived their ordinary lives, skipped breakfast every weekday. My mother left the house each workday, I think, at 6:15 a.m., drove the car to the bus stop in town, took the bus to Albany, and so on. But in the next room, now, my mother was pleading with my father:

"Why did you have to curse him with the evil eye? Why did you confront them? It's that—I'm worried. Are we so different? Sometimes I wonder why we ever moved here."

Was my mother just using an Anglo stereotype about Spanish-descended people? I don't know. The evil eye: a look or a glance capable of inflicting harm, an idea perhaps a thousand years old, even dating to biblical times, ubiquitous throughout Western culture. My mother might have been retreating to middle-class security, but in my childhood imagination then, my father, whose difference was powerful, was protecting me.

>+∘+<

My father's wanderings brought him through the New York City theater scene in 1967. Teresa had said both of them worked together on an off-Broadway production she described as "a precursor to *Hair*." My mother remembered Rene had worked on an off-Broadway production with Morgan Freeman, thus this production may have been 1967's *The Nigger Lovers*, which, despite the abrasive title, was a critically acclaimed play about the Freedom Riders and the early civil rights movement. The contemporaneous *Hair* debuted off-Broadway in October 1967.

I presume Rene's theater connections led him to a ski resort in New Hampshire, where he worked at a summer theater program. Shortly thereafter, he would turn up in Stowe, Vermont, also working for a theater program, and, where, in 1968, he would meet my mother. In later years, my mother and father often returned to Greenwich Village to visit. My mother used to tell a story to illustrate how well-known my father was in and around the Village. She'd be walking the streets with him, and they'd be stopped repeatedly by passersby, "Rene, how are you? Where've you been?"

Once, my mother tried to explain to me the idea of timelessness. I don't remember when, or how, it came up. It may have been in high school, or at home while on break in college, or in my early twenties: "Your father doesn't abide by our sense of time," she said, sipping her cup of tea. "His people dwell among the timeless. He thinks not in terms of hours and days but years and thousands of years. You'll understand someday." I later assumed she was talking about a popular but erroneous idea about Native Americans generally—and the Maya specifically: that they are peaceful philosophers, stargazers, calendar keepers. This view of the Maya would be rejected by the 1990s, but my mom had soaked up all the previous myths about the Maya, the sort of ideas she'd read about in magazines and the *New York Times*. Never mind that historically there were no Maya in the northern regions of Mexico from which my father's family hailed. Typically, in the notion of "Indian time," as we Americans have tended to think of it, Mexicans are laid-back and loose about time: it doesn't matter if we're late. Or, more simply, Mexicans are usually late. This view, let me say firmly, is false. As I write today, I recognize the subtle racism that my parents were steeped in and that coursed through our family life.

My mother told a story about a ski trip she and my dad made by car, years before I was born. I imagine through the windshield a snowy Vermont landscape. The windshield wipers pulse in an anxious rhythm.

My father is driving the car, my mother gingerly holding a paper cup of coffee. They were young: she in her late twenties, he in his early thirties. Her long, straight blonde hair spills out from beneath a winter cap with a tassel. Their downhill ski equipment, piled in the back seat, juts up behind them.

"Rene, stop the car." She grasps her temple.

"What's wrong?"

"I'm seeing something. Flashing lights. Stop the car."

But there were no flashing lights out there, on the road. At least, not yet.

In 1977, my parents bought the house in Middle Grove. An old farmhouse in the middle of nowhere, it dates at least to the early 1800s, before which point the records begin to get difficult to trace, my mother lamented, because of shifting property lines and the obscurity of early American handwriting. Among our neighbors were the writer Joseph Bruchac and the poet Kit Hathaway, both of whom knew my father in Ithaca. Bruchac would establish himself by writing compelling books for young people about Native Americans. Our families hung out some at parties, and I'd get together with his son, Jesse, who was my age. After I'd spent the day playing at their house, Joe gave me a ride home in his pickup truck, with Jesse and me holding on to a thick rope for security, the pickup bed buckling on the curves, the wind buffeting our hair.

Shortly after we moved into the old farmhouse in Middle Grove, my father began decorating. He brought home two large peanut sacks made of burlap—each sack was perhaps four feet high and three and a half feet wide. They had different messages printed on them in large block type: "Don't crush, fold, spindle, or mutilate." "Don't tread on me." He built wooden frames inside these sacks and hung them on the living room wall, and we had artwork in the vein of Robert Rauschenberg's assemblages. In the center hall, he hung a painting of an eagle, perched on a branch over a background of the red-and-white stripes of an American flag. I'm not sure if the message was patriotic, ironic, or deliberately ambiguous. I never saw him make any of these paintings. He brought them with him, presumably from Ithaca and New York City, likely having made them in the 1960s and early '70s. In Middle Grove, he was always making sculptures from found objects and displaying them around the house: scraps of iron and steel, hooks and bolts, levers and gears, springs and wires. He often collected these during trips to the town dump.

But we didn't truly live in the middle of nowhere. Middle Grove, our hamlet, was located a few miles from Saratoga Springs, then a city of predominantly Republican politics, which also happened to boast an arts community surrounding Skidmore College and its strong arts program, a summer resort atmosphere, artists taking advantage of Caffe Lena, the Yaddo artists' colony, the Saratoga Track (where they raced horses), and the Saratoga Performing Arts Center (SPAC). To the extent that we were bohemians, living on the fringes of Saratoga, we were dependent on a version of middle-class life that valued art. Our proximity to the larger cities of Albany, Schenectady, and Troy, plus the chance to take vacation trips farther afield, connected us to a wider world. We were a short bike ride from a small museum called Petrified Sea Gardens, whose displays reminded us our area once lay at the bottom of the sea.

My father brought several paintings with him when we moved into this new house. Some of them I caught glimpses of; others I would only learn about years later.

I suppose at root my father is an ordinary man. But I'm drawn back toward this sense of him as a bohemian artist. Then pushed back toward him as a decidedly unromantic failure. This split in my thinking even makes itself apparent in the mundane detail that my father didn't have a bank account—though my mother did. My mother always had more money than my father. My father chipped in, of course, to the household. While he had small jobs and carried cash, my mother had the big job. Big commute, "big" salary. The flip side was my mother had almost no free time. When I was a little older, in my twenties, I sometimes wondered if my father's lack of a bank account was attributable to his having been born in the Depression. While I never had the sense of our family lacking anything, there was a continuous sense of trying to scrimp and save.

The home in Clifton Park where I spent the first five years of my life, for example, had no running water, except for the leaky roof. Such a house—on the fringes, in the country, beyond suburbia—may seem to represent a place for the abject poor, the failures, the marginal, the down-and-out. But my mother and father saw a bohemian tinge in it. It was a choice—a glamorous, romantic, artistic one. It allowed my mother to pursue her creative writing and my father to purposefully wander.

In the late '80s, my father worked at a frame shop in Schenectady called the Ferguson Frame House. When I was an adult, Gabriela explained to me that picture framing was a typical job for artists to take, to earn money while making their art. My father's boss, Suzanne Ferguson, was an old friend of his, an artsy businesswoman in her fifties. She had an independent shop in a big Victorian house on State Street. The showroom smelled faintly of lavender, wind chimes rang on the porch, and new age music emanated from hidden speakers. Meanwhile, behind the counter, picture frame corners—frame samples—ascended the walls in soothing, decorative echelons. Suzanne commanded the showroom floor with entrepreneurial flair. She would carry orders, attached to their artworks, down to my dad, who worked in the basement.

Downstairs there was an orderly stockroom, its shelves and bays stacked with art supplies: matte board, Styrofoam, mailing tubes, paper cartons, core, rag. The damp air smelled of soap and adhesives. On the far wall, a doorway led down three steps to the workshop. There, fifteen-foot lengths of frame wood, called "stock," leaned upright in their bays, resembling a collection of giant wooden matches. In the center of the room was the island workbench, covered with brown paper that was splotched with glue and paint. Mounted on the workbench were hooks for hammers and two frame-cutting vises.

"Lay a piece of glass on the workbench," my father says, leaning over the work surface. He says to run the glass cutter along the straight edge, gently etching a line into the pane. "Set the glass on the edge of the workbench, and lightly tap it, and the piece snaps away."

As I hold the piece of glass, I feel the energy migrate along the score line. My father smiles with a glint of recognition. The plate breaks cleanly.

"I like the way the glass feels in my hands," I say.

He nods. It's a welcome connection. That afternoon, he goes on to show me the entire process of picture framing. But the thing I treasure most, even years later, is the feeling of the glass giving way, knowing it is under my control.

⟩┼••┼⟨

Sometimes my father showed me he *could* be in control. He was always there to pick me up from soccer practice, my afterschool job, or evening jazz band rehearsals. He did that necessary thing of fatherhood: he created a safe place for my sister Heather and me to thrive. He wasn't laid-back and loose about time.

Never in my experience was he late. He was like a machine, so reliably punctual I took it for granted. In fact, he was early—early to develop Alzheimer's at age fifty-four. When the phone rang, I guessed it might be Mom with news about Dad. When I was in my mid-twenties, we didn't talk on the phone much—usually we wrote letters. When I answered, and it was Mom, I joked about my being another psychic in our family.

On that Vermont ski trip, when my parents were young. Dad pulling the car over, stopping, Mom recovering at the roadside, then, getting underway again, only to find, twenty minutes later, on the way to the ski resort, one OC—"out-of-control trajectory," Mom said, explaining, as she put it, Dad's initialism. "Horrible car wreck, surrounded by police cruisers with their lights." Dad figured they would have put themselves in the path of that OC if the flashing lights hadn't occurred in Mom's vision, and he hadn't pulled over—*early*.

"I can't put up with it anymore," Mom said, her voice singeing over the line. I was in my Chicago studio apartment, on the phone. "He's a big man," she continued. "Still very strong. He struggled with me. Tried to hit me. I can't have him hit me. Of course it's not him. It's the disease. I'm just so sorry. I signed the paperwork for him to be admitted to Fort Hudson."

Fort Hudson, I knew, was the facility for long-term dementia care. Mom had talked about this, that Dad would need to go there someday. Now it was happening. She was increasingly afraid he might wander off and get lost, despite the aides who came each day, despite the locks she kept on the outsides of the doors. He was sixty-three years old; I was twenty-five. My chest throbbed with hurt, and I was ashamed of my reaction. I was torn because I wanted to respect my mother and wanted her to be safe. But I kept thinking: surely it must be too *early*. Timelessness. Indian time. He thinks not in terms of hours and days, but years and thousands of years. Surely in Mayan time, bohemian time, he's too early.

›‡•∙≺‹

I can hear my mother dropping key words: "He was such a wanderer—a bohemian. You didn't know him as he truly was." For her, these words were terms of endearment, respect, and acceptance. My parents refused conventionality, even as my mother worked a state job to cover for both of them financially, sacrificing her own vision of an artistic self to support her family. Of course the idea of his being a character in Richard Fariña's book was so important to her. My mother needed the myth of the bohemian more than he did. To her, his bohemia was a rejection of the norms and brutality of capitalism, and it allowed us—his family, his friends who cared to listen—to live under this system. Yes, it was a contradiction, but it also gave me a new way to understand "failure." "Failure" was a mark of pride.

When I was a young son, and he was first becoming hazy, I ran toward him, because I thought I could protect him. But I also ran away from him, afraid of the lifeless body he was becoming. Deep in the woods, far up on a gradual slope, two streams ran in parallel for years. There was my father, increasingly locked inside his body. The more jewels came out, the more he was forever trapped. His memories floated downstream like so much debris after a storm. He started volunteering as an aide for a memory care facility. I pitied him, I felt sorry for him, I was ashamed of him. Afraid I would become like him. I remember a life-size, black, ceramic rabbit with a dazzling, uniform glaze—one of his art projects from the memory care facility. It haunted me. I wanted to rid my father of this unacceptable illness, wanted to excise so many tangles and plaques from the brain. The more I pitied him and felt sorry for him, the more I realized I needed to be resolute, stronger than I'd ever been before, if I was going to survive the guilt and sense of loss. His early-onset Alzheimer's had deadly serious implications for me, his son. I would collect all the storm debris from the stream, and study it, and catalogue it, and sort it. There were so many particles and twigs and branches, and so much mud. I absorbed a lot of dirt. I started writing down stories, unable to distinguish the dirt from the shine. The only thing I knew: I needed to save everything, hoarding all of his discarded memories. He was my father, and he would not survive. His stream—with all its wreckage—was flowing to a place where it would join with mine. And what would happen then?

The Shape-Shifter

In Middle Grove, we lived a fifteen-minute drive from the town bars, along a winding and hilly country road. I spent a lot of weekends with my father in bars. My drinks were Shirley Temples; his were Scotch. My father drove the car while I sat in the passenger seat, the car swerving around corners, drifting onto the shoulder, and jerking back into the lane. He held the wheel in the straightaways, and then began to sway. His eyelids drooped, and his head dropped down, and then snapped to attention. I imagined how I would grab the steering wheel, kick my leg over, and stab the brake. I practiced this maneuver in my head, over and over.

My sister Heather gives a warm view of our father's behavior, saying that he was a "lovable drunk." My assessment isn't nearly so generous. Gone were his easy sociability, his gentle humor, his patience. He became irritable and impulsive, stumbling, slurring his speech—a stereotypical drunken menace.

He went to the bar, I suppose, for the same reasons so many people do: the impromptu social scene, the escape, the pleasure. When my mother asked my father to take me for a Saturday afternoon, he brought me to a bar. I'd glamorize it too much if I said bar-going was his only way back to bohemia. It wasn't that. Perhaps he went to the bars because he couldn't find pleasure doing "normal" Saturday things like home maintenance. He had companions and camaraderie at the bar. All his responsibilities faded away. His settled but tedious life was forgotten. He might even forget fatherhood.

》++◆+《

My favorite bar was decorated with ship's propellers, rope cargo nets, wooden barrels and crates, chrome bumpers, and scores of automobile license plates. I would sit at my own table, typically a dark slab intimating that this place was for serious and somber adults. Tonight, a dozen or so tables were filled with people, the after-work crowd, talking and laughing, eating wings and fries, having their beers.

I'd finished my drink, saving the sweet, red cherry for last. My father sat at the bar, still working through his course of drinks. The bright fruit in the bottom of the glass caught my eye, and I began slowly stirring the ice. As the rocks went round and round, the chase took on mythic proportions. The boy had left the ship, to make a pursuit in a small wooden boat, to harpoon the red sea demon lurking in the winter ice.

The boy, harpoon in hand, was caught in a whirlpool. The waves grew deep and an iceberg encroached. Poseidon appeared, changing the balance of power. The boy sent the harpoon through the red demon, and drew it up into the boat. At the table, the youth was eating a maraschino cherry the size of his head. The taste was acrid, foul, and sad. He withdrew the tiny plastic harpoon from his mouth, the flare scraping his tongue. Bringing the tip close to his eye, it was the elegant form of a trident.

》++◆+《

In my early years hanging out in bars, it was usual for my parents to meet after work on Fridays, for maybe an hour or two, getting dinner at the bar. So I automatically go to my table, sit down, and wait. My father brings me a drink.

A man comes in from the twilight, taking off his coat, brushing the snow off his boots, the melting ice smelling like spring. At the bar, a man orders himself a drink, and one for his son, whose face lights up. The father sits at the bar, his son at a nearby table, a short distance across the room. The man takes his time, occasionally talking with friends. Overhead, the decorations of cargo crates and automobile parts suggest travel, but the movement is, of course, all illusion.

The man turns across the bar, and sees, in a moment of marvel, his son is standing at his table, wildly thrashing the ice in his soda with a stirrer. The boy gulps the water, stabs the cherry, and pops it into his mouth. The man looks at the boy and raises his glass. The boy holds his own glass in his hands and drinks.

There were many other bars, many other names. *Uncle Joe's. Rich Man, Poor Man's. Quarters. The Hub. Tinney's. The Tin and Lint.* There must be many more. I spent a lot of painful time in bars as my dad's alcoholism grew worse and as I was growing old enough to understand the problem. As a child I never questioned whether bars were an appropriate place to spend time with one's father. Sometimes I connected or talked with my dad there, but I mostly spent time on my own. When I was younger, there was nothing particularly difficult about going to a bar. It was a place of adult entertainment and I found it interesting to glimpse this adult world. Of course I had no sense of how things could be different. I did not ask for a change. As I grew older and more curious about my father, it became more difficult to go to bars, even though I was quite comfortable spending time alone. Perhaps I remember going to bars so clearly because when I was younger those visits felt carefree, though when I grew older and more aware of my father's problem drinking, those visits became painful.

I think the reason I return to the difficult space of the bar is it represents for me the time when my father was still trying to be the man living against convention, even as the obligations of job and family put down predictable constraints. The bar represented a world he could no longer fully inhabit without neglecting some of his responsibilities. But I keep trying to surface these hard-to-trace, lifelike aspects of him: that easy sociability, that sense of comfort. The tiny sliver of generosity that meant, when my mother asked him, he agreed to take me rather than leaving me behind.

True, my father suffered from an illness that made his body demand drink. I learned this fact only later, when he was in rehab, and its implications would dog me all my life. If alcoholism was an illness, and influenced by genetics, it meant his behavior wasn't his fault or due to bad choices. Perhaps he was looking for something he couldn't find, and although he once may have been able to find it in a bar, he gradually may have reached the awareness he no longer could. If bohemia was such an ideal way of life, why did it require excess and self-destruction? As I learned from my father, bohemia could break down.

I can think of more pleasant memories of my father from earlier times—riding bicycles to swim at the Sheep Dip, building a fort from scrap wood, or helping him work on the car. But those memories were rare, and somehow my thoughts return to the steady, predictable rhythm of our escapes to those bars. They were simply part of my childhood story. Those were the places I spent time with my father, and I didn't know to ask for anything different.

⟩•••⟨

I wasn't riding in the car that day. While he emerged with just a few scrapes, the accident led him to give up drink. As challenging as that year was—and as much as that trauma stretched through my younger years—by the time I was an adult, I tended to minimize the history. The raw emotions of those days had lost their hold on me.

That summer, I'd come home on my bicycle, finding my father passed out on the freshly mowed grass of our front lawn, his lawn-mower stopped beside him. My stomach turned with revulsion at this public display of breakdown. I wanted to bring him inside, but my mother said to leave him be. It confused me.

Once, my sister and I sat in the back seat of the car while my mother and father argued. "Rene," my mother said, "you need to choose between your drinking and your family. Either you'll stop drinking or we'll get a divorce."

I could picture my father driving alone in the car, watching the road through half-open eyes. I'd been with him in the car so many other times when he'd been drinking. The engine runs in an efficient, quiet patter. The car rounds a curve, rumbling onto the gravel shoulder, careening back to center. The winding road blurs and warps. His head bobs down, eyes closing. *Bam.* The car slams between two trees. He passes out in the driver's seat. A trickle of blood seeps down his forehead. The car is totaled.

Several hours later, I walked with my mother into the police barracks in Corinth, fourteen miles north of Middle Grove, where my father was being held on New Year's Day, where he'd been taken for DWI. My father sat in a jail cell on a wooden bench attached to a wall. He looked weary, serious, and didn't smile. I stood beside my mother, my hands at my sides, suddenly aware of my purpose. If she was the queen, I was the knight, and she'd moved me into position. There was no anger or strong emotion between my parents as I feared there might be. My mother said to him only one thing, with coarse disappointment:

"Let's go."

>+++<

As an adult, I've picked up numerous anecdotes over the years supporting the idea that alcoholism *leads* to dementia. I myself avoid excessive drink. But what if genetics trumps alcohol use? One day, a friend's question catches me off guard. Are you worried about Alzheimer's and genetics? Do you fear since your father had the early-onset variant of the disease, you're more likely to get it? These are interesting questions. Some people learn about their Alzheimer's risk factor status through consumer genetic testing or think about getting that kind of test. I'm almost the same age as my dad when he started showing signs. Should I get tested for these risk factors? A genetic test strikes me as a high-tech means that could, potentially, be used to avoid the illness. But my gut response surprises me. I'm almost cavalier.

"I'll cross that bridge when I get to it," I tell my friend. I'm not in denial, but testing would only make me worry, without practical treatment options.

Still, the question lingers, so I ask my doctor. I've made an appointment to see her in person just to ask this question. Does the fate of genetics surpass personal behavior?

"The decision to get genetic testing is an individual, personal one," my doctor says, looking up from the laptop where she's taking notes. "With Alzheimer's, there's not much you can control if you carry a genetic risk factor. Plus, you've already had your children. No matter your genetic status, you can still make positive lifestyle choices: Don't be a hermit. Participate in social activity. Exercise. Avoid monotony. Keep it interesting."

I'm relieved. Her advice confirms what I've been doing all along—making good lifestyle choices. Plus, there's no need to test right now. But although her guidance about staying active is upbeat, it seems to avoid a deeper horror. It's a horror that has pushed me, throughout my life, to seek comfort in the arts. It's as if all of the lifestyle choices and genetics don't matter. I've arranged my life in an unusual way so as to accommodate this search for my father, to live only for the creative day.

Yet I've made some discoveries very late in the process. Through my writing practice, I realized that I incorrectly associated my father's erasure with failure. And now, as I'm beginning to consider more seriously the thought that I might succumb to this same disease myself, I've started to recognize a flaw in my thinking. I don't know what I believed. When the thief came, Rene didn't stand up for himself, and allowed himself to be robbed? He didn't notice when holes formed in his pockets and jewels fell out into the stream? These explanations made no sense. It was a huge thing for me to realize that *he didn't fail.* His dementia wasn't a failing.

Then what about his alcoholism, this behavior I always blamed him for? Even though I'd sat through counseling sessions with family members while my father was in rehab, and learned that alcoholism was a disease, and that my father had this illness because of his body chemistry, i.e., it was beyond his control, due to the genetics of fate, even though I'd internalized all of that, I still blamed him for how he treated me when he was drunk. Even though we were taught that alcoholism was a sickness and that we needed to support him and forgive him, I still struggled with deep-seated feelings of anger and blame. Could I forgive him this illness now?

Then what about the other issues I found, even before that? Was his earlier behavior—the womanizing, the serial families—also exempt from blame? Is that a gift I can give to him? Would I be too quick to forgive him? Is it enough that I stay true in my own relationships? What happens if I fail?

That summer after my father's crash, I visited him in rehab. This came after the charge of driving while intoxicated, all of which had brought a huge upset for our family, and prompted a glorious revolution. I sat on the campus grounds with my parents and my sister, and a friend of my father's from Ithaca from the 1960s, Phil, who was in rehab at the same time. Flower gardens and gently swaying pine trees surrounded us as clouds billowed across the sky. It was a comfortable day in late July. We ate picnic food: hamburgers from the grill with relish and ketchup, baked beans, and coleslaw. My father seemed so calm then. He was forty-nine, healthy and relaxed. He was *sober.* His hair was shiny black, his face clean-shaven, his eyes alert and attentive, and his body in good shape, as if he'd been exercising. This was the miracle I saw. He was a changed man. *Sober.* In my mind, it was as if he'd been through a heroic six-week battle against alcohol and won.

As he neared completion of his course of rehab, I looked forward to his return with great anticipation. But when he came home, I was disappointed. It was hard to start or sustain any sort of conversation. At first, my mother suggested that it was only temporary. Going through rehab had drained him, and it would take weeks for him to stabilize. True, he was sober, but the animated figure I knew when I was young was gone. Of the time when my father went through rehab, his friend Kit said, "He was fuzzy even then," and as an adult it surprised me to realize Kit was probably right. I'd hoped a new world would open up between my father and me, as if a cloak had been lifted. I would finally understand his intellect, the one I suspected was there all along. A conversation would finally begin. Of course I loved him, and tried to convince myself to love him more. But he never warmed up, never opened up, and my doubts about him, or underlying mistrust, never really went away.

One night, I woke to find smoke curling on the ceiling. My entire body became alert. Grainy smoke, too thick to be cigarette smoke. I told myself, leave everything, get out of the house. Of course as students we'd been drilled. It was a warm night in late June. I was fifteen, sleeping in cotton briefs and T-shirt. I started to choke on airborne particles.

Just get out.

Now I heard my father clattering downstairs, running water in the bathroom. I think I heard him hitting a bucket against a doorway. Something serious and unusual was happening, and I needed to act as quickly as possible. I left the bed, stopping to gaze at my bass guitar in its case. A quick decision. I took the bass and carried it downstairs and out of the house. I thought there was no real danger. This little fire would be put out quickly by my father with his bucket, and I was overreacting by taking dramatic action. But without a doubt the smoke was pooling rapidly. After I'd carried the bass guitar safely out the door, I went back upstairs to my room for the amp.

The episode I am describing happened over thirty years ago. In that time I've often reflected on its significance. This wasn't a dream or a book about a house fire. It was a real fire.

When we think of the symbolism of the house fire in English literature, it is an obliterating event, a total calamity, the absolute worst imaginable catastrophe. In *Jane Eyre*, Rochester's wife sets the house afire and dies after jumping from the roof. In *Fahrenheit 451*, the firemen deliberately go about burning houses down, the ones containing illegal libraries. In *Housekeeping* by Marilynne Robinson, her main character, to break out of her confining reality, burns her house down. As Catherine Addison, a professor of English at the University of Zululand, writes: "The English manor house set in its hereditary grounds was a visual sign in Victorian times of the power and confidence of the landowning class as well as the stability of the whole Imperial structure. The image of such a house on fire would suggest a breach of this confidence—an unthinkable vulnerability in the seemingly indestructible edifices of patriarchy and hegemony."

It's part of our culture to stand transfixed by the house fire—and be transformed by it. It's also probably true that most house fires aren't calamitous life-ending events. Once the blazes are extinguished, people turn corners. A hero may emerge from a house fire without serious harm, but still be changed by it. As for our family conflagration, I'd say it, too, posed a brutish test of confidence. When the night was over, I quietly felt that my father had made a terrible mistake, and that his failings extended to me. I can't lie about the feelings I had then. But as an adult, I tend to think I judged him too harshly.

That morning—was it four o'clock? three?—the smoke quickly became so dense it was dangerous. I shifted from thinking I'd overreacted by rescuing my bass guitar to thinking I hadn't reacted decisively enough. I took in the very real possibility that our entire house would burn down. The flames were out of control, lapping the walls and the ceiling. I began to imagine a total loss, our house turned to blackened ruins. I'd escaped from the house and was standing a good distance away in my underwear, my guitar and amplifier not too far from my side. When I grabbed these items, I wanted people to get the idea that music was important to me—even more important than finding a pair of pants. It was almost meant to be a joke. But now I was having difficulty keeping up the act.

My mother approached me while I was standing on the grass at the edge of the road while monstrous black smoke poured out of the house. It billowed from the living room in massive plumes. When the front door was momentarily opened, smoke poured out. My mother looked at me.

"Where is Heather?" Her face creased with worry.

"I don't know," I said, realizing I hadn't thought of my sister until now.

"Did you see her? Did you hear her?"

"No, I didn't go down there." My sister's room was at the far end of a curving hall. I remember the hallway running on and on, not just because my associations with it are from childhood, but also because it represented the grandeur of my family home, its infinite lengths, its nearly unreachable hiding places. It's also true that as an adult, when I returned, I found a much shorter hallway, a disturbingly logical layout, and everything in plain sight. This hall reached my mother's study, the guest room, and Heather's room—the only room we knew to be occupied. That night, the hallway snaked through a daunting labyrinth.

"I'll go look for her," I said, walking toward the house.

Apparently my father had left a cigarette burning on the sofa, gotten sleepy, and went to bed. At the time of the fire, my father had been sober for three years. Any mental fuzziness on his part must be attributed to the earliest signs of Alzheimer's or the lingering damage of alcoholism, years after he'd quit drinking. Throughout my life, I've associated his actions that night with his drunken self, even though the fire was not caused by his being in a drunken stupor. This incident happened long after he'd been dry. It was careless smoking due to his becoming, in thinking and action, increasingly fuzzy.

When I was growing up, we were surrounded by intimations of house fires: cigarettes, matches, lighters, blowtorches—the latter of which my father used for plumbing tasks and for starting fires in the fireplace and the woodstove. Our house had a woodstove, two chimneys, and three fireplaces. We had ashtrays in every room, not to mention the residual ash. Our house was covered in ash. It covered the tables, the newspapers, and the furniture cushions. From age ten my regular chores were splitting and hauling firewood. Of course, as schoolchildren, we were drilled to imagine fires, and performed them in our school like theater. We exited the building en masse while crouching student stage hands waved crêpe paper flames at our feet.

The night of the fire, the cigarette had begun to fester in the sofa. Soon huge flames licked the walls, reaching toward the ceiling, sending noxious smoke into the house. Someone called the fire department.

In search of my sister, I went upstairs in my underwear, T-shirt pulled over my face. I got about to the top of the stairs when my lungs and eyes couldn't take the poison. The smoke and the heat were so bad. That sofa was made entirely of polyester and other synthetic materials, and the smoke it produced was the worst kind. The fire was in the living room, and smoke was rising up the stairs toward my sister's and my bedrooms. Except my sister's bedroom was at the end of that winding hall. What happened to my sister? I couldn't get through the wall of smoke. I so badly wanted to keep going, but the pain was too much. The burning smoke was too harsh. I gave up, holding my eyes, going back down the stairs.

⟩⟨⟩⟨

Thus my father's attention was diverted from dropping buckets of water onto the source of the fire to making his way through the smoke to see what had happened to Heather. I stayed in my place with my mother out on the front lawn.

In a few minutes my father had reappeared.

"She's not there."

I looked at him, unable to hide my disbelief. Did he really make it down the winding hall to her? Or was he just saying that because he couldn't make it? I was so mistrustful, so much more than he ever deserved.

"Did you make it back there?" I asked, doubling down.

"Yes, I did," his patience tested. "She wasn't there."

The firefighters arrived.

With little fanfare, they entered the living room, blasted the burning sofa with fire extinguishers, then unceremoniously carried the sofa out the front door. I was beside myself; and when I saw the three men carrying down the front steps the charred carcass of the sofa, itself in the shape of a body, it was all too easy to imagine my father, dead, a victim of his last failure. They set the body on the far edge of the lawn.

In an essay, Addison writes about the "link between fire and knowledge," recalling the architectural historian Stamatis Zografos. I tracked down and studied works by both of them, trying to get at my own "sudden rush of self-comprehension," my feeling of powerlessness that accompanied the hour of the firefighters' rescue. Addison says that "fire burns with painful intensity through the surfaces of things and offers a shock to the body and mind that strikes down complacency and deception." I suppose I used to think that if I ever were in a house fire, I would be the rescuer. But I was stunned into idiocy. There was a stench of smoke, and scorch marks leading up the living room walls, but otherwise the fire officials thought we would recover. The house smelled terrible, but the damage was minimal. No one was injured. The house was declared safe. I stood there, nearly undressed, with my guitar, knowing I had failed to determine the whereabouts of my sister. My attempts at bravery and audacious posturing had all boiled down to impotence.

At this point, it was maybe four o'clock, and Heather, eighteen, arrived by car. She was way past our unwritten curfew. Apparently she'd stayed out late with friends. "What is going on here?" she asked, scanning the gathered fire trucks. "Is everyone okay? I can't believe it!" She broke my sense of stillness by giving me a hug. We were so worried about her, asking ourselves why she wasn't able to escape, and *she wasn't even there.*

⊱┄┄⊰

Looking back, I could have checked on her first thing, before the smoke had grown too insistent. I was so absorbed in myself and thinking only of my guitar. It's an embarrassment, although I don't think it surprised anyone that I had grabbed my instrument and amp first. Even in my own story, I picture myself as a rather self-absorbed jerk, unheroically standing around in my briefs, thinking chiefly about music, waiting for the real rescuers to arrive.

The center of this anecdote, as I look back now, is my father. I hesitate to tell this story, because for so long I had mistakenly categorized it in my mind under blame for him because of his careless smoking. As a teenager, I couldn't help but see a failure. True, he had recovered from alcoholism and was sober. This story may seem like an example of his "drunken self," but he'd been sober for three years. It's interesting to recognize the two likely causes behind the fire: one, the murky damages of alcohol use, however long in the past; and two, his present dementia, now becoming apparent to us. This episode is surely an example of his own increasing haziness. Despite which, he made it through the smoke in an attempt to rescue my sister. I couldn't do it. But he did. And probably all of my life I've never given him proper respect for that.

The Father Figure

I was at a bar in Chicago. Live jazz music was playing, and from across the room, Jen was approaching me. We had an auspicious beginning to our relationship: fireworks and chemistry, and even more important to me, a sense that we could make it work as partners. We started dating in the fall of 1996 in Chicago, having met, as we would tell our friends and new acquaintances many times, at the Green Mill in Uptown, a jazz club. Upbeat music played and the red lights of fire engines flashed and swirled around the room. We'd gone to high school together, had many friends in common, and later recalled that we each had crushes on the other but never had a chance to do anything about it. As if to bless our reencounter, the band's vocalist, named Elizabeth Conant, from Greenfield, New York, shrieked with delight when she heard that two other people from Saratoga were in the audience. Strobe lights flickered and syncopated saxophones played. We felt favored by the stars.

Jen was tall. I stood at a little more than six feet and she was just a couple inches shorter than me. She had an elegant posture, sturdy bones, it seemed, and she was from Saratoga, and we both had gone to Oberlin, and we were crossing paths, again. Jen was smart, interesting, poised, and had come to Evanston, Illinois, the suburb just north of Chicago, for graduate school in art history at Northwestern. In the weeks that followed, we spent many evenings talking late into the night. Summer would be coming soon, she said, and I sensed the change of light prompted her to ask if I would like to visit her family's house in Maine.

We first went to Vinalhaven, Maine, together in August 1997. It was because of Jen that I met George, her father, known to many as Doctor Jolly. Jen and I were living then in separate apartments in Chicago. I took a flight to Portland, Maine, where Jen met me at the airport. She picked me up in her turquoise Honda Civic hatchback. She had driven east from Chicago to Saratoga and was staying with her family for part of the summer, longer than I could afford to miss from work. From Portland, we drove north to Rockland, where we would take the ferry to reach the island of Vinalhaven.

We arrived in Rockland late at night, her little car packed full with our bags, which we planned to carry onto the ferryboat as foot passengers in the morning. We stayed just across the street from the ferry terminal, at the hotel called the Navigator.

>+••+<

First, the setting: Vinalhaven, Maine. An island off the coast of Rockland, Maine, an hour's ferry ride from the harbor on the mainland. Oceanfront. The smell of salt air. Sheep's Island hiding in the fog out on Robert's Harbor. The house, built in the nineteenth century. The view of the harbor from the kitchen and the deck. It was my first time there. I was twenty-six years old.

When I first met George, I saw myself as the one fetched by his daughter. I was, at best, her interesting plaything. My father, because of his illness, never had the chance to converse with me as an adult, as George and his daughter did. With them, I felt like a novice at adult conversation. George was the commanding and kindly interviewer. His gaze would go inside. I feared he would discover I was an imposter, someone of pretense and without substance who had come to take away his beloved daughter.

Doctor Jolly offered me a drink. Even though I declined, the mood was set: it was time for drinks. But George pivoted, dropped to his knees, fidgeted briefly with one of the lower cabinets, then took up a power drill, *voosh, voosh, voosh,* began taking the doors off the cabinet. He got up, left the room, brought in more tools—a radial saw, a tape measure, a T-square, and some lumber—got on his knees again, removed the cabinet doors, then the countertop. My perception of "this thing we are about to do" shifted. As George did one more adjustment, he found something else to fix, until I realized what he had set out to do was to remodel the kitchen. Not time for drinks, but for renovation. We heard that by the end of the summer he had built new cabinets and countertops for the cottage. I was astonished and humbled, thinking this work was something I could never do.

One reason I felt such warmth for Jen was our separate history of childhood visits to Maine. I truly loved going to the seashore as a child, but after my fourteenth birthday, we no longer went. By then, certainly, we were beginning to worry about Dad; meanwhile our mother, with quiet purpose, started planning the trip to Texas. We would miss the ocean, but hopefully find his family. One couldn't have everything.

Our visits to Maine during my childhood filled me with a fair amount of wonder. We would spend a week or two at Indian Point in the summer, eight or nine hours by car from Middle Grove. When we did go there, I found treasure: quartz, dead manta rays, quahogs, giant strands of sugar kelp, tiny snails. Several summers we did not go to Maine at all. But I still loved those memories from when I was four and my father built bunk beds in the back of the van for the long trip. As we reached Georgetown Island, outside of Bath, I was happily listening to the strains of Harry Nilsson's "Me and My Arrow" on the radio as the day grew dark. Through the windshield, the headlights caught the irregular shapes of hand-painted road signs, many of them made from pieces of driftwood. I drifted off to sleep before we ever arrived at the cottage.

In Maine, I can picture my father working on the *New York Times* crossword puzzle on the daybed in front of the picture window. The daylight from the sky filters through the cedar trees. Far down the hill, the waters of the Sagadahoc Bay ripple. It's a small, tidal bay that completely drains at low tide and you can walk across it. My father leans his muscular frame over his newspaper, his right leg crossed under the left. Speckles of gray dot his curly black hair. A scent of brine and evergreen permeates the cottage. Outside in the narrow country lane, I'm walking with my parents when a neighbor gives a warning like a whip crack: *hurricane.* This new word sounds like a punishment. The next day, the hurricane rolls in. I'm indoors with my family as the wind howls like angry giants and the house creaks and shudders. Spurts of water rush in through cracks in the walls. My father stumbles about, stuffing rags and bits of newspaper into gaps. The wind growls and the house buckles and thumps. My father tells my sister Heather and me to stay in one bedroom away from the windows. I push the door ajar to see my father crouching in the corner, making grunting noises, packing a hole with cardboard while the giant, white-capped waves lash inland along the bay. The curling tops of the waves seem so elegant, so beautiful, so cold.

><del>••</del><

The next day, trees lay fallen. Limbs and branches are strewn across the road. Thick sections of driftwood logs have been thrown across yards. We walk around the peninsula in dismay. I collect small pieces of wood that will serve as bridges for toy cars. My hobby horse, which was kept outside, has been carried away by the storm.

><del>••</del><

It's four years later, another summer, and we come down to the dock where Paul is waiting on his boat. The sleek, single-masted sailboat bobs gently at its mooring as Paul grins warmly, reaching over the rail.

Our family spends a lot of time near the water, but it's rare for us to go *on* the water. This requires the help of generous friends.

It's a day for vigorous, bracing sailing. Or so my father says. But the rough seas have hypnotized me. I climb into the creaking boat with trepidation. My unease gets worse as we bump our way onto the open ocean.

I stay inside the cramped cabin, fearing for my life as water laps over the windows. The boat is keeling so hard. I grasp the interior rail, a tight ache in my stomach.

My father says to come outside, it will be better for my nausea, but I don't believe him.

Through the doorway I can see him and Paul, a middle-aged guy with a short beard and faded denim shirt. He's the captain, it's his sailboat. My father, meanwhile, glows with a subdued radiance, curly black hair glistening, striped T-shirt flexing over muscles. He sits on the upward side of the boat, grasping the lines. A wave crashes in a spectacular plume behind him. As the wind shifts, my father and Paul switch to the other side of the boat, to counter gravity's pull. They call down for me to do the same.

What my father says about being in the open air: it's true. Years later, I'll look it up. Being able to see the horizon, and taking in the fresh air, would have been better for seasickness, than trying to stay inside the cabin with waves bubbling over the windows. At eight years old, I adored my father. Admired his physical health, his mental sharpness, his confidence with the ropes. But I was beginning to notice a pattern. He wants me to do the more difficult thing. To come outside, to brave the tossing surf, act more grown-up. Sure, *he's* strong enough to resist the dizzying motions. But I stay in my little compartment, betrayed by my body's balancing logic, stubbornly holding my own difficult position. I have only the thinnest sense of the open air, the horizon, the breeze, the sun, the clouds.

Moving ahead. It was twenty-seven years later when I became a father. Jen and I were in our midthirties when our twin boys were born. We named one of them Mateo, a recognizably Hispanic name, and named the other Joseph Rene, after my father, extending his memory, at least symbolically, into the future. Both of Jen's parents and their spouses came to the hospital to celebrate the birth. Our parents came down to our house in Brooktondale, near Ithaca, rotating on a weekly basis, to help us take care of the two infant babies. At the time of one of these visits, there was a huge snowstorm, but George and Caroline hadn't heard about it and showed up anyway. The power was out. We bathed the boys in the kitchen sink, their first baths. Another time, years before the boys were born, I was home in Saratoga, in the hospital, and George came to visit. It was a psychiatric hospital. My own father was fading from Alzheimer's. I was struggling with my own psychological torments. George helped me. I sat on a hospital bed, a tray of food before me, and George was trying to coax me to eat the food. But in my confusion, I literally thought the chicken salad was the flesh of my long-dead ancestors. It's a complicated story, but I'll try to speak briefly about it.

>+→+<

It was December. I was in my late twenties, experiencing a psychotic break. It happened out of nowhere. I had been visiting friends in Chicago. I was driving back to upstate New York, having lost sight of the fact that I had a return plane ticket from O'Hare and would miss my flight. I had taken my friend's car—without stopping to ask him. I had to get home to Jen. I pride myself on being able to say things clearly, but I've rarely been able to articulate what happened during those few days. The fears come back. I thought I was fleeing for my life, trying to escape from a hellish warzone.

I had lost touch with reality. I was gripped by what psychologists call magical thinking. I thought there was a war going on in the mainland U.S., everywhere around me. Signs and billboards seemed to bear special significance for me alone. Everything, everywhere, had a pervading sense of unreality. My sense of time passing was stretched out and distorted. You might think I intend to create some kind of drama, but I don't want there to be. There were multiple intertwined universes. My perception belonged to an immortal consciousness, but different versions of myself would die in different timelines. On the highway, I saw wordplay in every road sign. I'd see a truck with the message "Bob's Dirt and Stone" and I'd think Bob was an undertaker going to bury bodies in the war. I spent several days in a psychiatric hospital in Ohio.

As I understand it, the doctors found my case remarkable: how sudden was my break into madness, how quick and sharp was the recovery. Years later, one of my doctors gave me an article from a psychiatric journal. It was about "acute remitting non-affective psychosis." According to the National Institutes of Health, this group of conditions is not associated with a mood disorder such as excessive sadness or elation. It includes a broad set of psychotic conditions characterized by acute onset and brief duration. This means the change from a non-psychotic to a clearly psychotic state takes place within a period of two weeks or less, and continues for less than six months from onset to full recovery. The timespan of my own illness was even shorter.

In the immediate aftermath, I lived with painful memories related to having known my own disintegration. I'd already seen the end of my world. Clear and specific ideas rolled into my consciousness, visions of my entire world splintering into fragments. Big trucks with taunting images of poisoned food. Billboards that were scoreboards in the war. Time loops that didn't end.

At the time of my illness, my father had been institutionalized with Alzheimer's for about four years. He was coming apart, and I wanted to be the son who would pick up his memories, become the bearer of his life. But now I was coming apart too. I realized I literally might not survive, and the book—or the dream of writing one—wasn't the most important thing.

In the next fifteen years, I was revisited by brief episodes of frag-
mentation. If I had to count them, I'd say I had maybe eight or ten episodes of slipping out of reality. I know what it's like to lose awareness
of myself. These experiences gave me a close understanding of what it
meant for my father to have lost his selfhood, his personhood.

A big reason for trying to write a book about my father was to
regain control of an out-of-control situation. The book was a noble
endeavor, but even then, at times, it seemed like I was holding my
subject, my father and his illness, at a distance. Trying to gain control. I rarely gave in to the overwhelming power of my opponent: the
disease. But in those episodes, running in parallel with my father, I
had no choice but to give in. I was beaten by a self-devouring mental
illness.

As I recovered, I started to believe that there were in fact multiple
universes. The one I was in—taking charge of my father's memories
and legacy—was the only one in which I would survive. It was an imaginary notion, but it helped keep me going. My health history hasn't
always been at the front of my mind. It has stayed in the background,
lurking, a part of me, in remission. It's true that I've had a lifelong fear
of becoming ill like my father, or, more recently, like my mother. But I
need not have been afraid. Because eventually I would merge into the
universe, into the dirt, into the air. I would merge with my father. I
knew this because I had already done it. Not in a magical, supernatural
sense. But in the sense of an idea, within the limits of reason.

When Jen picked me up at the Portland airport in her car and we
headed up the coast together, I had relaxed in the passenger seat,
studying the map with the route she'd marked in highlighter. These
were happy times. We would visit her father in Vinalhaven; we would
have dinners in Middle Grove; we would walk in the woods surrounding her father's house. We were innocent of everything that would happen, given the weight of that first fracture, when the house of bricks
came falling down around us.

⟩⟨⟩•⟨⟩⟨

George aided me as a doctor, mentor, and spiritual guide, even though he was never officially my doctor. I discovered that his intimidating conversational gaze was simply deep attention and concern for you. When our twin boys came along, he passed along to Jen and me an old otoscope—a medical instrument with a lens and a light for looking inside the ear. It had a military green, dapple-textured, and worn case with a broken latch, and a frayed elastic string holding it together. We used this numinous otoscope many times during the boys' early years.

But if I'm allowed to have only one question for George, it's not about keeping psychologically healthy. It's about what happened to his marriage. Not something one plunges into in polite company. My doubts about my own father transposed themselves into questions for George. The doubts carried over. I doubted myself.

George was the family doctor: the doctor in the family, and the doctor *of* families. But there was a problem. The only thing I couldn't ask my family doctor was why he left his wife. He was married to my mother-in-law Penny until their children were teenagers, and they loved each other, they played music, gardened, traveled, and they separated. He remarried. I don't know if George ever told Jen why. I was afraid to ask any of them—George, Jen, or Penny. Their divorce, it seemed to me, was an act by George against Jen and Penny, but I couldn't ask. Only they would know the answer to why he left.

I wanted to ask George about his divorce when I felt confused by my own marriage, but I worried asking for clarity would imply something awkward about Jen. Perhaps the only reason for keeping a memoir of George in my notebook was my need for clarity, an acknowledgment that over the years he had become a father figure to me. My prolonged doubts about *my* father's failed marriages rearranged themselves into numerous questions for George, as if I could somehow protect myself from failure by obtaining the right answers.

I imagined George explaining various reasons why he left his wife: it was because the romance had fizzled, or the mounting arguments, or her inclination to control him, or the restrictions she tried to put

on him, and the more he would talk, the more I would see myself in
my relationship with Jen, and he would go on, and I'd be thinking,
I sympathize, and the harmony I supposed Jen and I had would be
broken. I would be hearing complaints that no one could bear to hear.

One of my favorite memories is being in George's motorboat on the
ocean, surrounded by dolphins. Blue water, clear sky, sleek glossy black
mammals with fins gliding up and out of the water. The animals are
beautiful and mysterious, and slip back under the surface as soon as
you begin to feel you have glimpsed them.

I've never asked anyone who's been through a divorce, "Why?" Perhaps
it's obvious, but it seems off-limits, no matter how well you think you
know someone. Even so, if my father were alive and in full possession
of his faculties and memories today, I'd probably ask him about his serial families, his marriages left behind. Why did these things happen?
My father and I never had the kind of intimacy that would permit such
a question to be answered candidly. Yes, surely I've come closer to my
father through my search. And certainly I was growing more forgiving.
But his motivations and justifications were secrets he'd taken to his
grave. At the same time, from what I'd learned, I was growing more
resilient in my own marriage, capable of weathering the minor slights
and misunderstandings of routine married life, as well as overcoming
the bigger potential pitfalls. I believe this was thanks to my search:
I'd been thinking about resilience in relationships all these years. My
mind occupied a place of penitence for my father's abandoned families, if such a position was possible, or believable. I became more cir-
cumspect, more tolerant. But I couldn't forgive him on behalf of the
wives and children he'd wronged. I could only forgive him for myself,
and for the most part he'd been good to me. There'd be something in-
sincere and unfair about *me*, the son who'd had him around, claiming
to have forgiven him. I didn't understand and couldn't forgive him for
leaving these wives and children, stranding them without support.

Another memory of Maine. This was the year of my bicycle accident. I was thirteen. That morning I was looking forward to another afternoon of sailing, because once again our friend Paul had invited us to go sailing with him. It was the only outing we'd planned since the last one all those years ago. But in a big upset, that morning I crashed on my bike. Broke my left arm, was in the hospital. When I finally got home late that afternoon, I sat around the house, all banged up, with a huge, swelling concussion over one eye, an arm in a sling and temporary cast, scrapes and cuts up and down my right side. My summer abruptly over, and the sailing chance—gone. I wish I could fix things that could've happened, that didn't happen, but I know that's impossible.

A few years later, I went to sailing camp, became an accomplished sailor. Was one of the bravest and most skilled sailors in the group. Could tack and turn about and inspect gear and tie knots with the best of them. I'm going to suggest that my adult self would ultimately triumph over these fears. Now, I picture my father with an eight-year-old boy in tow, and we're sailing.

We're riding in the boat, tossing on the surf, and I'm cowering inside the little cabin. "C'mon, Son, come outside," my dad says. And I realize, you know, let's give this a chance, maybe he's right. "Sure, Papa," I say, and go outside into the wind and sun. It's unusual for me to call him "Papa," so this must be an early childhood memory or a dream. I sit with my arm on the rail, lounging in the boat, my feet resting on a milk crate, and my dad and I have one of those long conversations about sailing technique and life and time. We're backlit by radiant clouds and lapis sky. Occasionally we're amazed by the spume dashing upside the boat. Papa interrupts me at various moments to point out petrels, terns, and cormorants. He's flipping through the Peterson guide, trying to help me understand the field marks. The boat seems to tack back and forth, almost in circles, for hours. By then, we've discussed pirates, dinosaurs, and religion. The origins of the twelve-month calendar. Rogier van der Weyden and the Plague. Equatorial telescopes and the Royal Observatory. Then we're adults, having sailed hundreds of times, and now old men, still boating and talking intimately after all these years. We look distinguished—this word I repeatedly use to describe my father, and myself, with a certain pride. Gray in the beard and hair, crow's feet at the eyes. My father looks at his watch, and then me, and says we better go in to shore. All this time, and I've just been craving a glimpse of him, a hint of clarity.

These conversations would increasingly populate my dreams—even now—with the result that I'd wake, knowing the feeling of the dream, the one where he's back after a long time of being away. I wonder why I haven't gone looking for him sooner. He tells me all about Leila and Helene and Teresa, and even provides glimpses of Coral from their early years, surprising me with details I've missed. He leans in, with a wry smile, and pantomimes nudging me from a distance. I reach back toward him, into the space between us. We're talking strategy while the wind changes, and watching the birds, all the while having one of those conversations I've always longed for but don't recall ever happening.

The Seer

Early in my search, Jen and I traveled to St. Louis to visit Gabriela. We found that her house, a classic brownstone, was filled with objects that hinted at her passions—cameras, photographic memorabilia, artworks, and quirky antiques. It was June 2001, a period of time you could almost describe as the last few months of the optimistic 1990s. In the comfortable furniture of her living room, we were looking at three-dimensional photographs through a stereopticon, taking in scenes of the American West: precipitous canyons, winding rivers, soaring pines. Her husband Guy was friendly and sensitive to the smallest social graces, on our first night barbecuing chicken and veggie burgers and serving a salad abounding with vegetables from their garden.

Back in her living room, Gabriela brought out a battered, tan suitcase containing a trove of documents relating to our father—identity papers which all the time I was growing up my mother had explained with frustration were lost forever: his birth certificate, social security card, and Army records—as well as personal letters and poetry. All this time Gabriela kept them in the very bag in which her father had packed them, as though he might return to collect them. The suitcase seemed to me a reliquary for her lost father.

I wandered in Gabriela's garden, admiring the sprawling green stalks and bursts of colorful flowers. We ventured out one night, enjoying a local specialty, frozen custard. During the day we visited the

Arch, and the St. Louis Museum of Art, where Gabriela served as a curator. I stood at the edge of the Mississippi and silently watched the passage of water.

A year or so later we all met up in Middle Grove. My mother led us across the living room toward my father's old room. It was summer, daytime. Gabriela, in a black-and-white dress, was accompanied by her husband Guy, in his usual jeans and a plaid shirt. Jen was there, too. Prior to our coming, my mother had brought out some of my father's paintings from his closet and set them on the floor, leaning against the walls. Here, in the living room of my mother's house, when Gabriela came to visit her father after his absence of thirty-five years, Gabriela crouched to study the artworks.

"This painting looks like my mother's," she said, holding it closer.

"There's no doubt," Guy said. "That's Helene's."

I looked over Gabriela's shoulder, studying the painting. I had never seen it before. Gold and copper concentric circles were layered like minute brickwork. The pattern, painstakingly executed, made a soothing optical illusion, in earthen brown and flax, recalling a Buddhist mandala. I took a deep breath. Involuntarily, my head turned aside, my vision a fog. These were the sharpest fragments to pass through my hands, to collect in my vessel. All a shattered mess. The streams were coursing down, and I knew I'd been following them all along, but couldn't believe they met here. This painting confirmed the connection between Helene and my father, the connection between Gabriela and me. It proved the existence of a hidden relationship, and now it was so exquisitely laid out. Layers of gold circled me. And now Guy was so confidently asserting again, "There's no question, that's her style."

I had sorted through so much rubbish in my search. Whether it was dirt or broken glass or empty beer cans I couldn't be sure, but the fragments were hard, bright, and razor-sharp. I had a feeling I was coming apart, going to faint. Then I straightened up. This hidden marriage was undeniably real, more so than Gabriela or I could say it was. Maybe it was because Gabriela and I were finite, temporal creatures, and the painting would live on after us. Rene had carried it with him when he left Helene and Gabriela. Now my mother would give the painting to Gabriela, and she would take it with her, back to St. Louis. It would remain intact when Guy died in 2011, at age fifty-three. It would still exist when Gabriela was raising their daughter, taking artistic photographs, and working as a curator in the art world.

In this painting, and its story, I could see my father alive, this breathing, moving person. The painting was a symbol, a work of careful execution, itself a mandala. I was going to survive—perhaps for decades. My father would not be so lucky. It was a beautiful thread, but a story would not help my father. He would inevitably die and I would live after him, with calluses and scrapes on my hands from the glass, knowing the stale odor of beer cans, my fingernails marked with the dirt from things I'd collected and sorted from the stream.

>+••+<

I see here, in a meadow outside the Fort Hudson nursing home, the elderly Rene, after Alzheimer's disease, with Gabriela, who has traveled to upstate New York to meet him. I follow a few paces behind with a camera, but I am shooting into the sun, not good for photography. Nevertheless, the image is emblazoned in memory.

We have, momentarily, escaped the institutional walls. The man and his daughter slowly walk in the meadow behind the nursing home, among the wildflowers alongside the Hudson River, near the railroad tracks. I sight the pair through the viewfinder of the camera, but the sun shines too brightly on the lens, making it impossible to take a photograph. The sunlit wildflowers surround the couple in a pale light. The man shuffles slowly and his daughter takes small steps. She turns her head toward him.

The two of them shift, dark silhouettes in the light. The father and his daughter wade through the tall grass. I slip forward, brushing through the goldenrod. Gabriela bows her head under the warm gaze of the sun. Rene and his daughter move along the path, holding hands.

The Underdog

I say this story started in Texas, but in many ways it also began in Mexico. The boundaries blur as we pass through Texas, learning of Teresa, on our way to Mexico City. While I'm living there, my travels around the country inspire me to write, but my subjects and my settings are nearly all in upstate New York. So now I'm traveling again. We're leaving our comfortable surroundings, and winding the tape backward. We're on our way back to Mexico.

In Mexico, I'm astonished to see many people, everywhere, who remind me of my Texas cousins, my father, and myself. But I'm not completely naïve. I don't blend in, and when I open my mouth, my accent, while intelligible, still marks me as a foreigner. While I'm working in Mexico, an email exchange with my father's friends Kit and Tom points to the hidden marriage with Helene. I find Gabriela and speak to her on the phone. Leaving the country, I collect all of my notebooks and place them in a box. Years later, I take them out again. Still, there's something about that first trip to the country, and especially that first eve of the Day of the Dead, that stays with me.

That night, in a scrubby field lit by streetlights, I meet a man dressed as a corpse. He peers out between bandages, beneath a surgical cap, fake blood dripping from his mouth. We're in a small town outside Mexico City, 2,600 miles from home. Yet there's something eerily familiar about him. It's his eyes. They remind me of my own.

"Hola, hundido," I say to the corpse. "Hello, sunken one." But I've
mixed up my Spanish. What I mean to say is "Hola, herido," "Hello,
wounded one," to compliment his Halloween costume. I'm surrounded
by partygoers, and they burst out laughing. "Hola hundido!" someone
guffaws. Hello, sunken one! The wit! I play along with their laughter
as if I'd intended the remark. The corpse walks across the field with a
brisk but limping gait, dragging bands of gauze in the dirt behind him.
Almost inexplicably I follow, assuming he's someone I've met tonight
through one of the revelers.

The dead all arise these days: on Halloween, by way of the United
States from European pagan roots; on All Saints' Day, the Christian
festival brought by the conquering Spanish; and on the Day of the
Dead, of pre-Columbian legend, when the Aztecs trekked to the Valley
of Mexico, following the marigolds that marked the way for the dead to
join the living on their journey. In Mexico, the holidays all blend into
one celebration that takes place from October 31 to November 2, when
death walks triumphant through the crowds.

〉┅┅〈

In the gallery, track lighting cast its beams over a large photograph of
the smoking Popocatépetl volcano. At the back of the room, a dozen
battered aluminum folding chairs faced a bare white sheet draped on
the far wall. Despite the rough edges, Jen and I were excited. We had
decided to start our evening here, where a friend of a friend would be
performing. This location had once been a bakery. The bread counter
was now a makeshift bar, with a sheet of paper reading in handwriting,
"Tequila," and beneath it, in smaller hand, "Cerveza." Wolfgang, the
performance artist, handsome with his sandy hair and icy blue eyes,
stood near the bar, holding a beer and talking to our American friend
Allison.

"Come and join us." Allison embraced me and I kissed her cheek.
She was twenty-one, a recent college graduate, a Fulbright scholar,

with pitch-black hair draping her shoulders. She wore an orange satin dress with a black, fuzzy neckline. "Can I get you something to drink?"

"Something without alcohol," I said, taking in the room.

"I don't know," said Wolfgang, shaking his head. "We have water upstairs." Apparently only liquor was served at the bar and water was kept elsewhere for the staff. Even as an adult child of an alcoholic, I allowed myself one social drink on occasion. Yet I went on frequent nondrinking binges when I felt the ghost of my father was near. In these pious, sober bouts of mine, I resisted alcohol when it seemed to be all around me. Water, with its life-giving properties, could ward off ghosts.

Before I ever visited Mexico City, I didn't realize how Popo—the patron volcano of Mexicans—towers above the horizon, easily visible to the twenty million people of the city. On the rare days when the sky is free of pollution, Popo and a ring of mountains come into view. I also didn't know that Popo is named for one of a pair of Aztec gods, figuring in a myth that is something of a love story. Or that because of a combination of familial and political troubles, Popo can be seen fuming, even when he sleeps.

>┼••┼<

The art show consisted of a series of abstract photographic slides of urban and natural settings, accompanied by live accordion music. Periodically, a red dress—just a dress—appeared on grassy lawns, or before gleaming cityscapes, or against the backdrop of derelict buildings. I found myself drawn in, feeling a sense of possibility but also melancholy. When the performance ended, I went up to the bar to ask for water.

"Te gustó el performance?" I asked the man behind the bar. He wore a T-shirt from the National Anthropological Museum with an illustration of Coatlicue, the Aztec goddess of birth and death. Coatlicue was a massive, blocky, stone deity with pointed teeth and, for a head, snakes made of blood. Unlike her, the man had gentle features and warm eyes. His hair spiraled down from his head in delicate, ebony curls. "Ah yes. It was very good," the man replied. He said his name was Ernesto and he told me they had water but had run out of cups. I must've made a plaintive face because he hunted beneath the bar and retrieved a small package of plastic cups and brought me a glass of water. As the liquid touched my mouth, I was grateful not only to Ernesto but to the goddess Coatlicue, who provides at the moment of taking away.

"Are you doing anything special to observe the Day of the Dead?" I asked.

"No," he said. In previous years he'd done so but tonight he was going to hang out at the bar.

"Does your family observe?"

"Yes, they've made an ofrenda and will stay up all night."

The ofrenda is the offering: the decorated altar and centerpiece of the Day of the Dead observances, set up for the holiday in houses, churches, and public spaces throughout Mexico. I told Ernesto I'd heard about a stunning traditional ceremony in Mixquic. You can take a microbus to avoid the traffic, and it was worth the effort. He said there was an elaborate festival, but the town was two hours away, it became unpleasantly crowded, and the traffic was terrible. I said instead I could go to the Zocalo and see the festivities in the central square. He said it made much more sense to go to the Zocalo. "You'll have a good time and it is not so far."

Sometime after the show ended, Jen and I left the gallery and made our way to a nearby restaurant. While we were waiting, Allison showed up in the company of Wolfgang and Ana. To my surprise, a young German artist named Tina, a brunette with light skin and sorrowful eyes, had come as well. I had never thought of myself as someone who picked up friends so easily, but that night our group was magnetic. We all crowded around the large table.

Tina was talking about her trip down from the United States through Mexico. She and her friend had met wonderful people. They stayed in houses because they didn't have any money. Once they were going to camp on the beach and people told them no, it isn't safe, come stay in our garden and you won't have any problem, and they were very nice and it was fine. Another time they came into a small town late at night and they were going to sleep in the car but it was so uncomfortable they asked a few people and they agreed to let them stay with them.

Tina mentioned she had an old Mercury Tracer that she had bought for eight hundred dollars. It was not so great a bargain when you had to make repairs once a week. The Mexican mechanics were resourceful, so much better than the Americans. The Mexicans frequently do not have the parts they need. They understand how the car works and often they have to devise their own makeshift parts. The Americans will say, we can't do this work, or we can do it for you but there's no guarantee, and all they want to do is replace old parts with new ones, without really understanding the problem. The Mexican mechanics won't even ask. They'll just do it. The Mexican mechanics could even bring Tina's car back from the dead.

Tina was thinking about driving down to Guatemala and she had space in her car and could fit one or two people. She didn't know how long she would be here in Mexico City.

"You know, Tina," I said, "we are planning on going to the Day of the Dead celebration in Mixquic. It's a very old pre-Hispanic tradition. There, it is said, they prepare a large meal and have drinks and go into the cemetery to hold a feast on the graves of the dead."

Jen said, "We've been told the families will remove the bodies of the deceased from the graves and clean them and feast with them."

"They take the bodies out of the graves?" Tina's eyes widened with disbelief. "Isn't that against every conceivable health regulation?"

"We want to find out if it's true," I said.

That night, I was intent on the Day of the Dead but everyone else was focused on the bustle and camaraderie of life. Tina huddled over her soup, slowly stirring. Wolfgang had said something funny and Allison was laughing. Jen was settling into a glass of wine. Time was going by very slowly, and still, we were going to be late for the dead.

We ate falafel, small round wafers that looked like sausages, and tacos arabes, hibiscus and squash blossom, Mexican sour cream, epazote, and chile serrano, wrapped in tortilla. This wasn't the Middle Eastern food of Chicago. As we collected our money and paid the bill, I looked expectantly toward the door, impatient to see the real Mexico, as if eating tacos arabes in Mexico City on the eve of the Day of the Dead wasn't all you needed to do to remember your dead.

⟩⟩•••⟨⟨

At the train station, we climbed the stairs to the platform, which was totally empty. Where was the crowd, the festive atmosphere? My watch indicated it was two minutes to midnight; the station clock said thirteen minutes after zero. We learned there would be one more train, the last train, but at least one more. Jen, Tina, Allison, and I stood on the platform, our hopes starting to waver.

Allison said, "I say we wait five more minutes, and if the train doesn't come, we should take a cab back to the center."

The night seemed to be coming to a close. The air was cooling rapidly. Time was passing slowly, and the smell of garbage lingered. At midnight the last train arrived. We caught the last train to the end of the line.

By the time we arrived at Tasqueña station my companions looked tired and my head was beginning to feel numb. I was frustrated by how long our travel was taking. I feared we wouldn't make it to Mixquic, but I couldn't accept defeat. It would take two hours. Why had we lingered so long in cafés and restaurants when we should've been looking for the dead?

In the metro station, an old man with a bristly gray beard was limping toward me, a human skeleton in a wrinkled suit and wide tie. He was telling me how to get out of the metro station to find the other bus route to Xochimilco—the key transfer stop on the way to Mixquic.

I had thought the skeleton was going to lead me only a short distance, but after walking for several minutes, I realized my companions had stayed behind and I was blindly following the limping reaper. In the streetlight I saw more fully his shabby suit and filthy, tiny baseball cap. I had crossed into the land of the dead and it smelled of rotting garbage.

The skeleton ran into the street, flagging down a bus that barely stopped. He threw his skinny arm up, grasped the handrail, and swung aboard the bus as it lurched away. I stood waiting in the cold, finally deciding to sit down. When the next bus arrived, the driver said no more buses ran to Xochimilco. I gave up, going back along a trail of stray dogs, around to a place where runners whisked by. They seemed to be in danger. I wound around into the station.

In the street we hailed a cab, a battered Volkswagen Golf whose driver wanted 300 pesos. "Two hundred," bargained Tina, who didn't have any money. The price was set at 230 pesos, an outrageous sum. We climbed in.

In the front seat, I pulled the seat belt over my shoulder, but there was no buckle to fasten it. The taxicab rattled and shuddered, the tires shrieked, and away we sped. The driver's side mirror was fastened with duct tape. The radio jutted crookedly from the instrument panel, blinking. Wires sprouted from under the dash. The speakers were throbbing and screeching unrecognizable Mexican pop music. The press of speed hit me as the road curved, slamming me against the passenger door. Jen reached forward from the back seat and touched my shoulder, comforting me like a benevolent spirit. When I looked back again, she had fallen asleep, no need to talk to anyone, except Tina and Allison were whispering back there. The clock was pushing one thirty.

"We have to pass through several towns," the cabbie said, listing off the towns. "You want to get to the festival?" he asked.

We came to the first town, where fires were burning in the streets. A group of shadows stood near a black-smoking blaze. An ecological zone was marked with a sign warning not to build on the land. The starry lights of the city stretched to the sky, a glimpse of beauty. The frantic pull and jostle of speed turned my stomach, slowing only for the topes—the speed humps—and then the tempo pulled at my intestines again. Through the window, I thought I caught a glimpse of Popo, a barely detectable silhouette against the sky.

At last, we arrived in Mixquic. In the narrow lagoon, islands with thin, decimated trees looked like they'd been mowed by grazing animals. The tree branches hung down as if weeping. Open gondolas, thin sleek boats with blue tops, plied the lagoon among the strewn trash. Signs for parking asked fifteen pesos and the lot was mostly empty. The crowds thickened as we came to the entrance.

On the street, at a market stall, I bought ponche, hot fruit punch with cinnamon and sugarcane floating in it, no alcohol. I walked through the market with my companions, amid the sepia streetlights and tables with neat piles of candy and bread of the dead. Skulls made of white sugar and chocolate fixed their plastic rhinestone eyes on me. I was drinking the sweet ponche. At two thirty in the morning, crowds milled along a curving dirt street, mostly teenagers with backpacks and jeans and young adults in their early twenties, many of them bundled in winter jackets.

I wanted to enter the cemetery, even though my head hurt. Jen went with me, Tina and Allison staying behind. As we entered, people scattered, and we found our way to the center, where there was a massive granite altar covered with marigold petals, candles, breads, stone skulls, bowls of incense, oranges, pictures of the dead, purple and white flowers, candy skulls, skeletons, statues dressed as the dead, and earthen ceramic goblets with drinks and sweets. Surrounding the altar were intricate, cut-out paper flags of many colors. I gazed at the altar with contentment and comfort, as if a friendly ghost visited me.

A woman in a black blouse, sweater, skirt, and tights sat near a grave site, her knees bent, her hand pressing her forehead, her face wrinkled with anguish and exhaustion, her small ofrenda of wine and sweet breads laid out between her and the gravestone. It was close to three o'clock. A young child clung to her mother. A group of teenagers in leather jackets and sweatshirts were singing to a boom box of American pop music. A handful of scattered mourners in formal clothes sat near grave sites. Some wore traditional Mexican-Indian dress, some women wore knit cardigans in solid blacks and whites with long skirts, and others wore Western business clothing. Jen and I left the cemetery and entered the cloister of the church.

In the cloister I saw a pile of old, worn, and broken bones. They appeared to be the indistinguishable bones of humans, left in a pile as if they once belonged to animals, no skulls, hands, or feet. The bones were picked clean, dusty and ashen. No posted signs explained them. At no point in the evening did I see any ceremony where they exhumed bodies of the dead, nor washed them, as I'd heard about. A polite Mexican man in a crisp white shirt, Fernando, met us in the cloister, explaining that the cemetery plots were given on twenty-year leases and if families didn't renew the leases the caretakers might remove the bones long after the leases expired. Some of these bones wound up in the ceremony. This explanation struck me as bizarre, sad, and alien, where the needy among the living were disturbing the dead.

Fernando, Jen, and I left the cloister and entered the chapel. I saw the beautiful ofrenda, the marigolds, the ivory-white candles, and the statuettes of skeletons. Burning incense filled the air. Fernando gave a learned explanation of the ofrenda. People put out offerings of sweet breads, candies, wine, and other things their loved ones would appreciate, all in the hope that the dead would return to the living. "And of course the dead do not come!"

"But they do return," I said. "The dead do not disappear." But I was speaking only to myself. Of course the dead do not rise. Fernando's words unsettled me. I was still troubled by the idea of how to convene with a father who was a ghost but who wasn't dead.

In Mexico City, they leave derelict old buildings standing. History is not everywhere pushed to the margins by innovation and progress. They even keep old cars running. Twenty-year-old Chrysler New Yorkers and patched-together Volkswagen Golfs hum along, a striking difference from the North, where winter, salt, and rust—and desire for the new—claim many of their brethren. Pre-Columbian ruins echo an earlier civilization. Half of the scholars of the country, including those not of indigenous descent, spend their time digging up ancient Mexico, digging their fathers out of their graves. Even in this country that had been abandoned by a father who could not remember, unearthing and excavating form part of the scenery. Driving around the country, I saw archaeologists everywhere, digging. You couldn't throw a rock without hitting one of their tents. Mexico is not a place to suppress problematic emotions. It provokes them to rise to the surface. People celebrate a holiday dedicated to commemorating the dead. Pre-Columbian ruins and archaeological parks evoke layers of human history. Modern speed and tumult compete with ancient quiet.

In the small hours, two of Fernando's friends, Luis and Mauricio, joined us and we sat under a sloping tarp and ordered drinks and quesadillas. I vividly remember eating quesadillas and drinking ponche and conversing about Mexico's place in the world. But I had also spent the night waiting for my father to make an appearance in memory, to return from the dead.

It was approaching four o'clock in the morning. Fernando and Mauricio stood up to leave, and I exchanged numbers with them. "You will stay until sunrise?" Fernando asked me, and Luis asked rhetorically, "Why stay here until sunrise when it will take two hours to get home?" The roosters near the tent began to crow. The first microbuses began to sputter and clatter around the corner. We climbed aboard one of them to get back to Tasqueña station.

The sun was coming up and ordinary Mexicans who did not take the day off were boarding the buses on their way to work, appearing calm and refreshed. I had unintentionally stayed up all night. It felt like magic, bumping along on the microbus, heading toward Mexico City as the orange-gold sun burned on the horizon. I leaned against the window, weary and euphoric in its glow. Jen reminded me that it was important that we be happy, not sad, on the Day of the Dead, as whatever state in which you find yourself, your visiting dead will be, too. You want them to be happy for the day when you are all back together again.

>+→+<

At that time, my father had been living with Alzheimer's for more than twelve years. A thief had been stealing his most valuable possessions, trapping him in a nearly helpless body. My father could no longer speak, and I could never be sure if he recognized me. Seeing the Day of the Dead festivities for the first time, I found dark comfort because they were a way of approaching my grief over losing him. All around Mixquic, a fabulous party was going on. There was all this excitement. People danced, live funk rock reverberated in the distance, and people drank sweet drinks and talked and laughed.

That eve of the Day of the Dead still strikes me as a night of transformation. Men and women in their best clothes brooded in a melancholy state at the graves of their loved ones while all around them partygoers lived it up, inside and outside the walls of the cemetery. I couldn't let go of this contradiction. I'd spent a night as a ghost, meditating on death in my own private time, drifting back and forth between the underworld and the place of the partygoers. I'd found a place where I could mourn this father of mine who wasn't dead but was nearly lost.

>+→+<

Ten years later, I was back in Mexico, arriving by car in the early evening in Angahuán, a typical Purépecha town of dusty streets, few cars, many horses, and houses with traditional wood plank construction. My friend and I asked a man on the street for directions to our hotel.

The man's name was Calletano. He wore a cowboy hat and leather chaps, and struck us as knowledgeable and quite charming. He said he could guide us on horseback to the volcano. When we expressed hesitation about making the excursion on horseback, he said not to worry. These horses were easy to ride. "In fact," he said, "son automáticos." We agreed to meet him and the horses at eight o'clock the next morning in front of our hotel.

The horseback journey began gently enough, but I soon was stunned and fearful at the steep and rocky trail we were descending, from the town toward the fields. Even so, the horse was sure-footed and proceeded carefully. The guidebook had warned us about how hard the wooden saddles would be, and how strenuous the journey on horseback was. But it all seemed a small price to pay to find adventure and to witness the grandeur and awe of nature.

I won't lie. My experience of riding in the saddle was difficult. However, I believe we in the modern world all too easily create for ourselves the illusion of security, of life without risk. And it can come to feel rather empty.

I had romantic ideas about volcanoes in Mexico. My first trips were framed by my reading of Malcolm Lowry's *Under the Volcano*. Artists and writers throughout the nineteenth and twentieth centuries have stood beneath the volcanoes of Mexico and paid homage to them. Volcanoes were beautiful beyond belief, powerful, destructive, and unforgiving. By analogy, Mexico was a place of the beautiful, of the inhospitable, of downtrodden and proud people, and a crucible of political revolution. The volcano is a source of dramatic power, destructive, transforming, a symbol both political and mythic.

In all, we spent five hours on horseback. We went for two and a half hours to reach the base of the volcano. We took forty minutes on foot to ascend the volcano, and a half hour to circumnavigate its rim, taking pictures and surveying the view. It was fifteen minutes back down—skittering and sliding on our feet over the loose, gravelly slope. On our way back, we stopped at the Templo San Juan Parangaricutiro, a ruined church rising from the lava flow, a site spectacularly evocative of the powerful forces of nature and myth.

When my mother called to tell me my father was dying, I still blamed him for his drinking, for subjecting me to his risky choices, even though that was years ago and he'd recovered. It made no sense that I still felt feelings of blame, because he'd changed. That day, on the phone, my mother said he was having difficulty breathing. I had to piece together what was happening apart from the words. There'd be no last words or final reconciliation with a man who had been unable to speak for a decade and who almost certainly couldn't understand me. On the phone, my mother didn't want me to be alarmed, didn't want me to drop everything and leave. The nurses were working to make my father comfortable. He might not live long now. He might turn around. It was hard to say. I lived 205 miles from the nursing home in Fort Edward, a drive of almost four hours.

"I'm coming," I said. I could hear my father's labored breathing, a persistent bullfrog groan. *Hwaw, hwaw, hwaw.*

"Don't hurry, don't rush," she said. "He might not make it. I don't want you to be disappointed if you don't get here in time."

}+•+{

On our way to the volcano, I kept thinking of lost time. It may've been that our riding on horseback created a sense of the timeless. We made few stops, perhaps lulling us into a mesmerized state. To view the landscape as we did, on horseback, evoked the journey a visitor might have made in the 1940s. The idea of time travel came to mind, even as I rode the horse, disorienting me further with its paradoxical connotations. While I was riding through the extraordinary landscape, my mind was all too eager to believe I was time traveling, creating a sense of awe, but perhaps damaging any logical capabilities of memory.

The Paricutín volcano is indeed an extraordinary natural wonder. Its name might sound like Popo, but it's a far smaller volcano, located eight hours away by car. Even so, the lesser mountain poses some very challenging hiking and rewards with dramatic vistas. Paricutín was formed rapidly, dramatically, and brought before the eyes of the world through the new tools of mass communication of the 1940s such as photography, print journalism, and radio. The villages below and the surrounding agricultural region suffered the loss of millions of dollars' worth of crops and productive farmland. They were forced to reposition themselves economically, to change their way of life virtually overnight to survive.

As I write, I realize that I'm attracted to the volcano in part because it is a natural metaphor for an alcoholic father: unpredictable, growling, about to fall asleep or explode, looming over our family life. The alcoholic is a victim who has no power over his fate. He's a victim of his body chemistry, of cheap and abundant liquor made available in a market economy, and a victim of the indifference of others. Even though, in life more generally, I didn't feel I myself was out of control, I kept asking myself, do I have control over my fate? Somehow, in riding that trail to the volcano on a horse that I couldn't control, on an animal that decided for itself when to walk and when to run, it made me feel I had no control, but it brought me closer to the father I'd lost.

In upstate New York, when my mother telephoned to tell me my father was dying, I left the office, got in the car, and picked up a few things from home: a set of clothes, a toothbrush, some mixed nuts, an apple, and a bottle of water. I began driving east toward Fort Edward and the nursing home where my father was taking his last breaths. It was about one o'clock in the afternoon. I was alone in the car with a radio that barely worked. No music of any kind.

I crested a hill and saw a beautiful sunset. The sun was behind me, but reds, blues, and violets spread across the horizon. I thought, if I don't get to see my father today at least I can say I witnessed this stunning sky. He's leaving me during this godlike sunset. The breathing of my father's ghost softened. My chest tightened with anguish but tears didn't come. I had an overpowering thirst. I drank from the water bottle, thinking of Coatlicue, the goddess of birth and death, of creation and destruction, the woman who gave birth as she died. The goddess provides at the moment of taking away.

I arrived at the nursing home in Fort Edward and walked inside the institutional walls: white tile, fluorescent lights. My mother met me in the hall and we hugged. She said we can take as much time as we want with him. The nurses understand and will give us all the time we need. Are you ready to see him?

We sat down in two chairs opposite my father's bed. My father lay with his arms over his chest, his face ashen, his lips apart. He had held on through a seventeen-year struggle with Alzheimer's. He could no longer swallow his food. I suppose the nurses had moved him one last time to his bed. He'd stopped breathing, and died.

>+•+<

When we reached the base of the Paricutín volcano, it's true, the dormant volcano we found was much like the father I knew in his late period, after the gray ash of Alzheimer's had fallen: docile, contemplative, quiet, seemingly wise but with no words of his own, his memories borne by those survivors around him. Steam rose from vents in the ground, whispering in warm shallow breaths, reminding us of his former potential. If the active volcano is a symbol for the disruptive side of the alcoholic father, then the dormant volcano is a symbol of the man asleep, after the fire, under the sentence of dementia.

It shouldn't surprise me that I find the idea of the volcano at the center of my sense of Mexican identity. Volcanoes are, of course, a common part of the Mexican landscape. Here, at the Paricutín volcano, was a part of my father I wished I'd understood more clearly—not only the growling misbehavior and bad choices involving alcohol, but the other side of the volcano, the sleeping giant ready to awake and fight for political justice, with a sudden, explosive show of force.

Back in Angahuán, when we returned to our hotel, in the parking lot I snapped a photograph of our little car, our conveyance home. Then, as I looked across the street, framed by the parking lot gate, beside our automatic horses, I saw a billboard for Alcoholics Anonymous. I took a picture of that, too.

When I think about all of those times and adventures in Mexico, the one thing that keeps coming to mind is the fact that the volcano was still steaming as we walked its rim. And how loose and pebbly was the ground as we slid and slipped back down. It all seemed so happenstance and indefinite while we were there, but also eternal. Now I was the one who could travel through time. In fact, I had been doing so all along, hiking alongside the old stream, even crossing through it, picking up strands, bottles, splinters, driftwood, old watch straps. I had thought I was picking up only shards, but the truth was I was also picking up gems: amethyst, ruby, sapphire, diamond. In an instant I could return to any moment in the past. I was the vessel for my father's memory, even though a story wouldn't help him, and someday eventually I would die too, but this vessel would survive us. People would know he was a living, breathing man. We could travel to any point in time together, and people would know he was alive.

When I was fourteen, my father woke me up in my bed in Middle Grove, his body a silhouette, his face a charcoal drawing. The bedside clock said one at night. The room was filled with shadows. "What is it?" I asked. "Did you forget? I told you I'd come for you," he said. "Get dressed." I stumbled around in the darkness, turning on a light. Glooms appeared in the window. I went downstairs, where my father placed a heavy pair of binoculars with a cloth strap around my neck. We pulled on our winter coats and hats and went out into the November night, our breath steaming like the vapors of ghosts. The stars spread across the sky in a stunning landscape. We stood, and I was shifting my weight back and forth to keep warm, lifting my head toward the atmosphere. The meteors began to fall like rain. I felt as if I needed to grip the ground, as my father, the Earth, and I plowed through space, crossing the meteoroid stream through the heavens.

ACKNOWLEDGMENTS

This book is part of a larger project carried out over more than twenty years. One aspect of the project was the search; another was writing a book; and another was publishing various chapters from the work in literary journals as personal essays.

The opening chapter, "Return of the Lost Son," appeared in the *North American Review* 301, no. 3 (2016).

"The Motivator" is based on an essay, "Mother, Father, Memory, Me," which was published in *Stone Canoe* 8 (2014).

"The Bohemian" is based on "My Father, Wandering," which appeared in the *Hopkins Review* 16, no. 1 (2023).

A passage from "The Underdog" was published in "The Meteor," *Stone Canoe* 17 (2023).

Another passage from "The Underdog" was published in "My Own Lost Mexico," *North American Review Online* (2017).

ACKNOWLEDGMENTS

With these words, I thank:

Kate Blackwood

Bridget Meeds

Joanne Hindman

Jeremy Schraffenberger

Annette Levine

Steven Yao

Robert Moore

Eric Maxon

Phil, Carolyn, and Olivia Ortiz

Jay Rogoff, who has been my de facto literary mentor since the earliest problematic drafts for this project so many years ago, and who has been unfailingly forthright and honest in his critiques, and persuasive in his praise and support, and who has helped me grow so much. I've looked to him as a father.

Phoebe Peter Oathout

Dora Malech

Molly Beer, for her support, charm, and witty remark that my old manuscript of Mexico was like a country I hadn't visited for a long time.

David Guaspari

Eleanor Henderson

Edward Hower

I appreciate the overall support of Jennifer Savran Kelly.

Thanks to the many informants, friends, and family who appear in the book: Kit Hathaway, Tom Hanna, Aunt Jeanne, Aunt Mary (in memory), Tío Gus (in memory), Gloria, Minnie (in memory), all of the aunts, uncles, and cousins, Heather, Teresa, Helene (in memory), Gabriela, Barbara Bernstein, C. Michael Curtis, Juan Felipe Goldstein.

Heartfelt thanks to Leslie Cook for details about Leila, Renee, Andrea, and Mark.

Additional thanks to:

> Honor Moore at the New York State Summer Writers Institute at Skidmore, who probably doesn't remember me because I was so bad, and who nevertheless took me seriously and gave me some advice that I'll always remember.
>
> And to James Miller for all the comments, critiques, and humor.
>
> Jennifer Brice at the Colgate Writers Conference.
>
> Joseph Bruchac for the wonderful, brief, and insightful letter about my dad.

I don't recommend trying to write a memoir of your father if you were sixteen and he was fifty-four when he began showing signs of early-onset Alzheimer's disease. It is very hard, and so much seems lost. Yet this search has given me meaning after the catastrophe. I hope I've demonstrated that supportive networks can be built just by talking to people who knew your loved one. All is not lost. Draw on the memories and works of others. They are your medicine.

"conversations . . . longed for." See Maxine Rosaler's brilliant and irresistible short story "Zeldie Hamlisch," which appeared in *Prairie Schooner* 95, no. 4 (Winter 2021).

An anonymous peer reviewer at LSU Press helped strengthen this manuscript in so many ways. Thank you.

To Joseph and Mateo, themselves long aware that I am also a son.

I offer sincere appreciation and love to my mother, Coral Crosman, and my late father, J. Rene Gonzales. I can only give you the honor of following so closely in your footsteps.

And to Jennifer Jolly. This book is as much yours as it is mine. We did it.